Twayne's English Authors Series

Sylvia E. Bowman, *Editor*

INDIANA UNIVERSITY

Jerome K. Jerome

TEAS 164

Jerome K. Jerome in the "rorty young days" of Three Men in a Boat,
by Solomon J. Solomon. Permission of the National Portrait Gallery, London.

Jerome K. Jerome

JEROME K. JEROME

By RUTH MARIE FAUROT

Elbert Covell College, University of the Pacific

Twayne Publishers, Inc.   ::   New York

Library of Congress Cataloging in Publication Data

Faurot, Ruth Marie.
Jerome K. Jerome.

    (Twayne's English authors series, TEAS 164)
    Bibliography: p. 189.
    1. Jerome, Jerome Klapka, 1859-1927.
PR4825.J3F3   823'.9'12   73-15938
ISBN 0-8057-1291-7

MANUFACTURED IN THE UNITED STATES OF AMERICA

To my father and Agnes
AND
The nieces three:
Anne, Jeannette, Mary

ABOUT THE AUTHOR

Ruth Marie Faurot received her A. B. from Park College, her M. A. from the University of Kansas, and her Ph.D. from the University of North Carolina, where she studied with J. O. Bailey, working on nineteenth-century fiction.

Miss Faurot's double interest is in Victorian literature and the teaching of literature to students of other languages. Miss Faurot has taught English in Kansas and Nebraska. At Inter American University in Puerto Rico she taught English and American literature and linguistics. She is at present a professor of English at Elbert Covell College, University of the Pacific.

Professor Faurot has written articles on Swinburne, Hardy, Stevenson, and Sterne. Her present interest is in the New Humorists of the 1890's. She is at work, now, on an anthology of the New Humorists and a book on W. W. Jacobs.

Preface

The name Jerome K. Jerome evokes from many the nostalgia of pleasant reading; of the comedy in *Three Men in a Boat— To Say Nothing of the Dog;* of the melodrama in *The Passing of the Third Floor Back;* and of the delight of shared opinions of *The Idle Thoughts of an Idle Fellow.* Popular in the 1890's, the Edwardian period, and the first third of this century, Jerome's reputation survives in the memory of that catchy name, the titles so usefully quotable. During Jerome's lifetime, *Three Men in a Boat* ran to more than three and a half million sales in English, in addition to American piracies and foreign translations. It has become a part of the various classics series, Everyman, Penguin Paperbacks, Collins Classics, Time Reading Program, and has appeared in a handsome edition of the Folio Society. His works have retained their popularity in foreign countries, meriting three dissertations in German. A 1956 translation of *Three Men in a Boat* was published in Minsk, Russia. The works, aside from some of the maudlin plays, are quite readable today. A recent collection, *The Humorous World of Jerome K. Jerome* (Dover Publications, 1962), distills by its selections from the journalism and books the charm of his light moments. His reputation will probably rest on his humorous works. Yet there was a serious side to Jerome K. Jerome, and he was a spokesman for a large segment of the Victorian and Edwardian times. He knew well the lower classes. He particularly understood the discouraged individual, and he saw the good in the wrongdoer. His idealism became a message in his late novels. His plays form part of that movement in the drama usually represented by the problem plays of Ibsen and Shaw. In his essays, though he assumes the pose of the idle contemplator of the busy scene, a man of the world, his sympathies break out for the poorly paid—the actors, the messenger boys, the occupants of down-at-the-heel boarding houses.

Jerome K. Jerome produced some twenty plays, though only a dozen or so have been printed. They were, for the most part, stage successes with long runs. *The Passing of the Third Floor Back,* starring Forbes-Robertson, has become a stage classic.

As a successful editor of the magazine *The Idler,* Jerome numbered among his contributors Mark Twain, Bret Harte, Rudyard Kipling, George Bernard Shaw, Israel Zangwill, Sir Arthur Conan Doyle, and W. W. Jacobs. Less flamboyant than *The Savoy* or *The Yellow Book,* the magazine represents another side of the esthetic decade. As editor of the weekly *To-day* Jerome speaks out on politics, the German military, and peace. Travel notes were a specialty of the editor, and *Three Men on the Bummel,* describing a bicycle trip through Germany, is still read.

Two ideas dominate Jerome's works. One is the idea of idling. The word itself intrudes into his titles. Busiest of writers, his own life had necessitated a struggle that must have made "idling" a dream indeed. Idling provides a contemplation of life—the dream and the contentment. Yet the contemplation brings to the front the second theme, the pity for the failures. "I love the fierce strife," he writes, then adds, "I like to watch it." And of other writers watching he concludes, "What we really want is a novel showing us all the hidden undercurrent of an ambitious man's career—his struggles, and failures, and hopes, his disappointments and victories. It would be an immense success. But then not one novelist in a thousand ever does tell us the real story of his hero." Jerome K. Jerome in that paradoxical idling has shown us, if not the hidden undercurrents of the hero, at least the shared experiences of Everyman.

With all his popularity, Jerome's work has merited no critical assessment. This book intends to survey the considerable output of his forty years of writing. Although the order is chronological, this organization falls happily into genres, as his career progressed from lighthearted essayist to concerned dramatist to angry novelist. Jerome's comments from *My Life and Times* provide primary criticism, and these comments I have distributed along with my own assessments. I have summarized plots so that readers may understand the discussion of Jerome's works. I have, however, quoted extensively, particularly from his humor; for his fun should be read, not explained.

My hope is to send the reader back to the works of Jerome K. Jerome. His humor and his pathos still speak to today.

RUTH MARIE FAUROT

Elbert Covell College,
University of the Pacific

Acknowledgments

Thanks are due to the following for permission to quote from the works of Jerome K. Jerome: to Dodd, Mead and Company, New York, and to Miss E. M. Frith and Hutchinson and Co., Ltd., London, for passages from *All Roads Lead to Calvary;* to Hodder and Stoughton Ltd., London, for permission to quote from *My Life and Times;* to Dodd, Mead and Co., New York, and Cassell and Co., Ltd., London, for *Anthony John;* to E. P. Dutton and Co., New York, and to J. M. Dent and Sons Ltd., London, for permission to quote from the Everyman Edition of *Three Men in a Boat* and *Three Men on the Bummel;* to the National Portrait Gallery, London, for the reproduction of the Solomon J. Solomon portrait of Jerome K. Jerome on the dust jacket.

I shall always be grateful to Dr. Rachel Palmer and friends from Inter American University of Puerto Rico for intellectual stimulus. At the University of the Pacific, I owe gratitude to Dr. Clair C. Olson and to Dr. A. J. Cullen for encouragement and a faculty study grant. I wish to thank Mr. James Riddle's library staff for invaluable help. To Mr. and Mrs. D. W. Garber I owe a debt for the finding and giving of rare books.

To Mrs. Constance Cullen and Dr. Anne Passel my thanks for kind criticism and the listening ear.

Contents

Chronology

1859   Jerome Klapka Jerome born May 2 in Walsall, Staffordshire, of Nonconformist parents; the father, a partner in the iron works, soon lost money in coal mining.

1862   Family moved to London, where Jerome received some schooling after the National Education Bill at the Philological School at the corner of Lisson Grove.

1871   Father died. Family moved to Finchley; Jerome's school days ended when he was fourteen.

1873   Began to clerk with the London Northwest Railways Company at Euston. Mother's and aunt's deaths and sister's marriage left him alone. Tried acting in theatrical companies in London with modest success; joined a touring company.

1877-   With stage companies for three years; returned penniless to London. Tried journalism; taught for a few months.

1885   "On the Stage and Off," serial essays appearing in *The Play*, then in book form.

1886   "Stageland" articles in *The Playgoer* (then book form). *Idle Thoughts of an Idle Fellow*, in *Home Home Chimes*, then in a book.

1887   *Humors of Cycling*, one chapter and the preface, Jerome's.

1888   Three plays, *Sunset*, *Barbara*, *Pity Is Akin to Love*, and also *Fennel*—an adaptation of François Coppée's—presented in London. Marriage to Georgina Henrietta Stanley.

1889   *Idle Thoughts of an Idle Fellow; Three Men in a Boat.*

1890   Trip to Germany followed by *The Diary of a Pilgrim-age*.

1891   Produced *Woodbarrow Farm*. Christmas book, *Told After Supper*.

1890- A number of plays—*New Lamps for Old; Ruth, The*
1896   *Prude's Progress, The Rise of Dick Halward, Biarritz*.

1892- Editor with Robert Barr of *The Idler*. Contributed a
1897   series called *Novel Notes; John Ingerfield and Other Stories*; The Idlers' Club; *Sketches in Lavender, Blue*, and *Green*.

1893- Began a weekly illustrated paper, *To-day*, which ran
1897   until a libel suit forced him to sell out, with costs of 9,000 pounds.

1898   *Second Thoughts of an Idle Fellow*.

1900   *Three Men on the Bummel* records a cycling trip through Germany.

1901   *The Observations of Henry*.

1902   Wrote and produced *Miss Hobbs*. *Paul Kelver*, his autobiographical novel.

1903   *Tea Table Talk*.

1904   *Tommy and Co.*, his second novel.

1905   *Idle Ideas in 1905* (in America, *American Wives and Others*).

1908   *The Passing of the Third Floor Back*, successful play; *Fanny and the Servant Problem*, comedy; *The Angel and the Author*.

1909   *They and I*, another novel.

1911   *The Master of Mrs. Chilvers*, a play on the woman suffrage question.

1913   *Esther Castways*.

1914   *The Great Gamble*, a play closed by the bombing.

1915   Jerome joined the French ambulance corps.

1916   *Malvina of Brittany* (in America, *The Street of the Blank Wall*).

1917   *The Celebrity*. a successful comedy.

1919   *All Roads Lead to Calvary*, polemical novel.

1923   *Anthony John*, a novel of northern industrial England.

Chronology

1925 *The Soul of Nicholas Snyders*, a short story dramatized.

1926 *My Life and Times*, memoirs.

1927 Honored in Walsall; made Honorary Freeman of the
borough.

1927 Died while traveling in Devonshire; buried in Ewelm,
Oxfordshire.

1928 *The Passing of the Third Floor Back* performed in St.
Paul's Cathedral.

CHAPTER 1

The Passing of Jerome K. Jerome

I *Family Influences*

JEROME K. Jerome was a Londoner from the time he was four years old. He loved the excitement of the city, its boardinghouses and slums, its clubs and its theaters. Yet he liked to remember that his mother was Welsh and that his father traced his ancestry to the Scandinavian invaders. Jerome's father, also a Londoner, had been educated at the Merchant Taylors' School; trained as an architect, he had been "called" to the Nonconformist ministry. He preached at several Congregational churches and besides drew the plans for the buildings. He began married life as a well-to-do farmer in Devonshire, the seat of his ancestors, and, building his own farmhouse, had brought to it his bride, Margaret Jones, the daughter of a Swansea solicitor. Financially he failed in all that he tried, in the silver mines in Devonshire, in the coal mines at Walsall in Staffordshire, and as a merchant in London. He called himself one of the world's unlucky ones, Jerome recalled, and in his father, Jerome saw the idealist lacking the power to carry out his dreams.

In the mining town of Walsall on May 2, 1859, Jerome Klapka Jerome was born, the last of four children; he had two older sisters and a brother Milton, who died when Jerome was a baby. The name "Clapp," Jerome's father's middle name, was the ancestral family name. The son's middle name was borrowed. The Jeromes had taken in the Hungarian refugee General George Klapka while he wrote his memoirs of the Hungarian insurrection, and "Klapka" both honored the distinguished guest and preserved the Danish name.

The mixture of Danish and Celtic blood in Jerome's family, as well as the dual nature of his father, figure prominently in Jerome's serious works; for he repeatedly writes about the struggle between the dreamy idealist and the man of action. The Clapp family crest shows an upraised arm grasping a battle ax, a sign of action, accompanied by the motto "*Deo omnia data.*" Significantly, in Jerome's last novel, *Anthony John*, the hero's family name is "Strong'nth'arm"; and the protagonist, who has succeeded as a business man, comes back "to rule and guide—to make the land fruitful, in the new way";[1] he succeeds in his idealism only because he has first proved what the man of action can and cannot do.

Although Mr. Jerome lost his money in a venture in the coal mines at Walsall, he was much respected for his ministry in the Congregational Church. Yet Jerome's memories of those early days in the North Country, recorded in a sketch called "Silhouettes," are grim: "My memory travels to a weary land where dead ashes lie, and there is blackness—blackness everywhere. Black rivers flow between black banks; black, stunted trees grow in black fields; black withered flowers by black wayside. . . . When the sun shines on this black land it glitters black and hard; and when the rain falls a black mist rises toward heaven, like the hopeless prayer of a hopeless soul."[2]

Jerome's father went to London to try to recoup his finances in the wholesale ironmongery business, and almost two years passed before he sent for the family. Forced to move to London to a life of poverty, Jerome's mother idealized her early Welsh and Devonshire days; and her fairy stories and superstitions gave Jerome a love for fantasy. If the details of his autobiographical novel, *Paul Kelver*, are correct, his first attempt as a writer was to compose fantasy—stories full of princesses, fairies, and heroic rescues. The practical side of him found that the public liked comedy; but because the idealistic strain remained, his works contain incidents of visions and portents derived in part from the accounts of his mother's and father's life.

Poverty and hard times marked the boyhood home of Jerome K. Jerome and caused strain in the relationship of his parents. Genuine love between them, however, remained. In more than one of Jerome's novels, though, the discrepancy between the ideal of the young love and the sometimes ugly struggle as it fails becomes a theme. In *Anthony John*, Mrs. Strong'nth'arm says, "I often used to lie awake beside my man and wish I could always think of him as he was when I first met him: brave and handsome, with his loving ways and his kind heart. I saw him again when he lay dead, and all my love came back to me. A girl thinks, when she marries, that she's won a lover. More often she finds that she's lost him. It seems to me sometimes that it's only dreams that last."[3] The father died when Jerome was twelve years old.

Jerome's parents had been eager to preserve their gentility, and they were delighted when the National Education Bill had made it possible for the boy to enter the Philological School at Lisson Grove when he was already ten years old. Jerome, who lived at home, made the long trip by catching the morning seven-fifteen train after a fifteen-minute walk. "So I breakfasted at half-past six, and caught the seven-fifteen," he writes in *My Life and Times*. "The seven-thirty would have done it. But my father's argument was: 'Better catch the seven-fifteen. Then, if you miss it, the seven-thirty will still get you there in time. But if you catch the seven-thirty, then if you don't you're done.'"[4] Jerome made friends, fought schoolboy fights, learned the streets of London.

At home, the strict Nonconformity of the family had its influence; and though his parents were pious, Jerome never considered his restrictions nor his poverty to be reasons for bitterness. Religious dogma he seems to have questioned from childhood. Practically all his serious characters in plays or novels argue about the nature of God. *The Passing of the Third Floor Back* has a religious theme. *All Roads Lead to Calvary*, published in 1919, suggests by its title his preoccupation with Christianity; and *Anthony John*, his last work, preaches a type of Christianity derived from Tolstoy.

Poverty, too, plays a major role in his serious works, and of it he writes not only with understanding but with first hand experience. With his father dead, fourteen-year old Jerome took a clerk's job with the London North-western Railroad at the Euston Station and supported himself and his mother and sister on twenty-six pounds a year. Overtime pay, though, was twopence halfpenny an hour; therefore, he often worked overtime for spending money so that he and his sister Blandina might go to the theater—a form of entertainment that much troubled his mother. He recounts his mother's reaction to his sister's first invitation to the theater in *My Life and Times*:

> My mother was much troubled, but admitted that times might have changed since she was young; and eventually gave her consent. After my sister was gone, my mother sat pretending to read, but every now and then she would clasp her hands, and I knew that her eyes, bent down over the book, were closed in prayer. My sister came back about midnight with her face radiant as if she had seen a vision. *Babel and Bijou* I think had been the play, at Covent Garden. It was two o'clock in the morning before she had finished telling us all about it, and my mother had listened with wide-open eyes; and when my sister suggested that one day she must adventure it, she had laughed and said that perhaps she would.[5]

Jerome idealizes this situation in his autobiographical novel *Paul Kelver*; in it, both the father and mother of young Paul excitedly attend their first stage performance. The poignant scene in the novel represents both Jerome's own love of the theater and his sadness about not having shared it with his parents.

A year later, Blandina, marrying, moved North; and Jerome, alone, attended his mother in her final illness. Then, confronted with a terrible loneliness, he painfully made his way at the age of fifteen while moving from boardinghouse to boardinghouse. These difficult times he recounts in *My Life and Times* in almost the same words that he uses for the boy in *Paul Kelver*: "The two or three years following my mother's death remain in my memory confused and disjointed. The chief thing about them was my loneliness. In the day time I could forget it, but when twilight came it would creep up behind me, putting icy hands about me. I had friends and relations in London who, I am sure, would have been kind, but my poverty increased my shyness: I had a dread of asking, as it were, for pity. I seem to have been always on the move, hoping, I suppose, to escape from solitude."[6]

II   *The Actor and Journalist*

For entertainment, as well as for the financial boost, Jerome began to take parts in the productions of theater companies. Success of a minor sort tempted him to quit his clerkship to take to the road with the traveling actors. His venture earned him little money, and he returned to London after three years on the stage. He was penniless, but he had gained a knowledge of people and had accumulated experiences that provided material for a first successful series of essays, "On the Stage and Off." Moreover, the knowledge of the theater that he had acquired undoubtedly formed the groundwork for his success as a playwright. "Though I say it myself," he writes, "I think I would have made a good actor. Could I have lived on laughter and applause, I would have gone on. I certainly got plenty of experience. I have played every part in *Hamlet* except Ophelia. I have doubled the parts of Sairey Gamp and Martin Chuzzlewit on the same evening. I forget how the end came. I remember selling my wardrobe in some town up north, and reaching London with thirty shillings in my pocket."[7]

At loose ends, Jerome agreed to his landlady's suggestion to share quarters with another of her boarders; and in this way he met George Wingrave, who later became the "George" of *Three Men in a Boat*. Wingrave encouraged Jerome to become a journalist. After he tried "penny-a-lining" for a time, he became a school master for a few months. He could have become secretary to Herbert Spencer, but his sister feared that he was on the way to perdition from the theater, journalism, and now association with Herbert Spencer, so he rejected the offer. For a time he became secretary to a builder, a broker, then to a solicitor.

During this time Jerome had been writing stories, plays, and essays; but it took time for recognition to come. His first publication was a romance, "a sad thing about a maiden who had given her life for love and been turned into a water-fall, and over the writing of which I had nearly broken my heart."[8] It was accepted by *The Lamp*, a magazine that, Jerome says, expired soon afterward. Jerome discovered that such subject matter was not popular; and taking advantage of his experiences with the provincial stock companies, he submitted amusing accounts to a penny paper called *The Play*,

a new magazine edited by Aylmer Gowing, a retired actor.
The sketches appeared in book form in 1885 as *On the
Stage—and Off,—The Brief Career of a Would-be Actor.*
The book sold well, and Jerome basked in journalistic success. Acquaintance with other young writers followed, and
his social life expanded. There was bicycling, a new sport
in those days; rowing on the Thames; and playgoing at night.
He also joined a group called the "Old Vagabond Club,"
whose purpose was to discuss literature and drama. They met
in the rooms of the blind poet, Philip Marston; Coulson Kernahan, Dr. Westland Marston, Carl Hentschel, George Wingrave, and Pett Ridge formed the group. The acquaintance-
ship had been made during their attendance at theaters;
and calling themselves "pittites," they began to meet after
the plays to discuss them. The group expanded a year later
into the "Playgoers' Club," which eventually achieved a
membership of five hundred, including most of the
playwrights and actors of the turn of the twentieth century.
The club gave dinners for such guests as Sarah Bernhardt and
Henry Irving, and its members were honored with the occasional presence of the Prince of Wales and Princess Alex-
andra. Jerome K. Jerome was elected the first president of
the group, which continued well into the twentieth century.

The magazine *The Playgoer* emerged from the enthusiasm of the club, and to it Jerome contributed a series of articles called "Stageland," illustrated by Bernard Partridge, a
prominent illustrator for *Punch.* These essays, describing
the type parts of "The Stage Hero," "The Stage Comic Man,"
"The Stage Lawyer," and "The Stage Villain," pleased the
public; and they form today a valuable record of those bare
years of Victorian drama before G. B. Shaw, James Barrie, and
Oscar Wilde.[9]

Jerome contributed during the same years to the magazine
Home Chimes a series called "Idle Thoughts." Published
as a book, *The Idle Thoughts of an Idle Fellow* (1889), the
essays sold enormously well. Jerome could now afford to marry. In St. Luke's Church, Chelsea, with George Wingrave as
best man, Jerome married Georgina Henrietta Stanley,
the daughter of Lieutenant Nesza of the Spanish army. After
a brief honeymoon, they took a flat in Chelsea Gardens. De-

scriptions of a bride and groom's first experiences in house-keeping appear more than once in Jerome's writing. Recalled with affection, they undoubtedly derive from his own experiences.

By this time Jerome had, in addition to journalistic work, published his two books and written four plays. Three of these were performed in 1888 and 1889—*Sunset, Pity Is Akin to Love*, and *Fennel*. He had also been studying to become a solicitor, but encouraged by his wife, he decided to devote all his time to writing. "She is half Irish," he wrote, "and has a strain of recklessness."[10] The recklessness paid off. Sitting in the top-floor flat in Chelsea, Jerome wrote *Three Men in a Boat*. "I did not intend to write a funny book, at first," he writes. "I did not know I was a humorist. I never have been sure about it. . . . There was to be 'humorous relief'; but the book was to have been "The Story of the Thames," its scenery and history. Somehow it would not come. I was just back from my honeymoon, and had the feeling that all the world's troubles were over. About the 'humorous relief' I had no difficulty. I decided to write the 'humorous relief' first—get it off my chest, so to speak. After which, in sober frame of mind, I could tackle the scenery and history. I never got there."[11]

The characters George and Harris were founded on fact, for Harris was Carl Hentschel, a young photographer, and George was George Wingrave. The three men had often gone bicycling and on boating expeditions together, and their banter and jokes find their way into both *Three Men in a Boat* and later in *Three Men on the Bummel* (1900), which records their cycling trip in Germany. *Three Men in a Boat* became a best seller; it was pirated in America; it was translated into twenty-three languages; and it still remains a popular work, appearing in various popular classics series. The Heath simplified-English version has taken Jerome's funny story to wherever English is taught as a second language.

Jerome, who next turned to editing, began with Robert Barr an illustrated monthly, *The Idler*, which appealed to a more robust set of readers than the contemporary esthetic magazine *The Yellow Book*. The necessary money was Barr's; the title, Jerome's. Jerome ran a popular feature entitled "Novel Notes" and a breezy column, often a colloquium, called "The Idler's Club." Contributors to the magazine were then, for the most part, young and unknown: G. B. Shaw, Marie Corelli, Sir Arthur Conan Doyle, Israel Zangwill, W. W. Jacobs, Eden Phillpotts, Coulson Kernahan, and Robert Louis Stevenson. G. B. Shaw, Aubrey Beardsley, and Richard LeGallienne contributed not only to *The Idler* but also to Jerome's next publication, the weekly illustrated journal *To-day*, which he alone edited, concurrently with his work on *The Idler*. *To-day* ran from 1893 to 1897, and Robert Louis Stevenson's *Ebb Tide*, a serial in the magazine, sparked some of its success. Jerome wrote a series called "Characterscapes," and "his clever editorial notes upon current political and social happenings were brilliant pieces of journalism."[12]

To-day was killed by a libel action which ended in a draw, but the costs of the suit forced Jerome to sell both *The Idler* and *To-day*. Still only in his thirties, Jerome returned to playwriting. *Miss Hobbs* (1902), produced in America, became his first money-making success, playing one hundred and fifty-eight performances. Liberated woman made for good comedy at the time. In the same year, Jerome's first novel appeared—*Paul Kelver*, an autobiographical story depicting the sensitive growth of a boy. It was Jerome's favorite work—perhaps his best. Never contented to live in London's West End, Jerome found himself returning to East London and rediscovering the favorite haunts of his boyhood. His *Paul Kelver* recreates those scenes. Critics who had, on the whole, been unfavorable in their comments on much of Jerome's work recognized the skill of this novel. Having proved himself a successful novelist, he returned to writing plays and more of his humorous sketches.

By this time famous, Jerome toured the Continent and lectured in America on three different tours. His attack on lynching, in Chattanooga, produced disagreement; but otherwise he and America pleased each other. While in the United States, he traveled extensively and was in San Francisco, the guest of the historian George Bancroft, the week before the great earthquake. At Salt Lake City, the Jeromes were guests of a leading elder of the Mormon Church. New Orleans, Atlanta, Niagara, Florida—his speaking tours covered the states; but very little of his impressions of Americans, except some essays on the independence of American women, make their way into his books in the fashion that his observations of the Germans, French, and Italians do. However, while in America he approached David Belasco with his script of *The Passing of the Third Floor Back*, an adapation of his previously published short story. As a result of this encounter, one of the most popular plays of the time was produced. With Sir Johnston Forbes-Robertson playing the lead, the enormously popular play added to the fame of Jerome, who had previously been acknowledged as a humorist. The Christlike character of the Stranger in the play projects an appealing idealism that has kept the play in production to the present.[13]

In the comic vein, *Fanny and the Servant Problem* (1908) played successfully in New York, but it failed in London, where it was panned by the critics. As a musical comedy, it ran for four seasons and, translated, played all over Europe. On the other hand, *Cook*, or *The Celebrity*, which Jerome did not expect to be particularly successful, received raves from the critics in London. *The Master of Mrs. Chilvers* (1911), on the current question of women's franchise, won much applause and is one of Jerome's best plays.

Jerome's daughter Rowena not only played in his play *Esther Castways* with Marie Tempest in the lead but also performed as Stasia, the slavey in *The Passing of the Third Floor Back*, when it toured the provinces. The 1914 war came just as Jerome's play *The Great Gamble* opened, and unfortunately it had a German setting. In *My Life and Times* Jerome writes: "How the coming of the Great War was kept from us common people may be instanced by the production of my play, 'The Great Gamble,' at the Haymarket, six weeks before the guns went off. The scene was laid in Germany. One of our chief characters was a dear old German Professor. German students, in white caps, sang German folk songs and drank Lager beer. We had incidental music, specially written, in the German style. . . . For a solid month,

we rehearsed that play without a suspicion that the Chan-
celleries of Europe were one and all making their secret preparations to render it a failure."[14]

When the war came, Jerome, too old to enlist, fretted over
his inability to be more actively helpful. The solution came
from an encounter one morning with an old friend who was
dressed in a uniform supplied by the French Army, which was
"less encumbered than our own with hide-bound regulations.
Age, so long as it was not accompanied by decrepitude, was
no drawback to the driving of a motor ambulance."[15] Jerome
volunteered as a driver in a company of twenty Britishers,
and his memories of the war form a chapter in *My Life and
Times* (1926), but they also serve in a significant passage in
All Roads Lead to Calvary (1919), in which Joan, the heroine, becomes a war nurse.

Jerome had also served as a special government envoy to
Washington to help speed America's entry into the war. After
the war, Jerome devoted considerable time to peace movements, for he shared, in general, the opinions of the group
associated with Norman Angell. He had, even before the end
of the war, made speeches—along with Ramsay MacDonald,
Dean Inge, Israel Zangwill, the Snowdons, and Lord Lans-
downe—appealing for a negotiated peace. His health had
been somewhat injured by his work in the ambulance corps,
too strenuous for his age; and he had finished, as he said,
"cured of any sneaking regard I may have ever had for war."[16]

After the war, Jerome wrote two novels which were deeply
concerned with the working out of a practical Christianity
that was based on the idea that an incomplete God needed
the love and aid of man to make a more perfect world. *All
Roads Lead to Calvary* (1919) makes use of a young newspaper woman as heroine; idealistic, she is tempted in her pur-
suit of a career. *Anthony John* (1922) fittingly concludes
Jerome's fictional works because it returns to the boyhood
of young Strong'nth'arm who was from the manufacturing
area; successful in business, he renounces his wealth in
order to serve in the poverty stricken area of his origin.

Reflecting upon his career from "Poverty to the Knight-
hood of the People," Jerome recorded his memories in the
delightful *My Life and Times* (1926). A rambling chronicle,

it nevertheless teems with fascinating anecdotes of his acquaintances. Among the many unknowns who were his friends, there are a considerable number of famous people: Mark Twain; G. B. Shaw, who slept so hard there was no use trying to roust him out; Sarah Bernhardt, who slipped away offended from a large dinner party because no one had recognized her; Sir Arthur Conan Doyle, who was conceited about his knowledge of languages and who got his fellow-traveling companions into trouble. Jerome's sense of humor delights; half clown, half preacher, he comments on his sixty-odd years of experiences. A most readable autobiography, it remains the prime source of information on him and his works.[17] Indeed, the 1928 biography of Jerome by Alfred Moss relies largely upon Jerome's own account of his life. Better organized than Jerome's account but lacking its wit and fun, Moss's work records the last days of Jerome, the public honors given him in his birthplace of Walsall—the "freedom of the city" and a public banquet. It tells of the death of Jerome while on a trip to Devonshire with his wife and his daughter. He died of a heart attack and is buried in the churchyard at Ewelm, near Wallingford, where Jerome and his family had lived for some years. Mrs. Jerome lived until 1938. When their only daughter Miss Rowena Jerome died in 1966, she bequeathed two portraits of her father to the National Portrait Gallery: one of Jerome in "the rorty young days" of *Three Men in a Boat* is the work of Solomon J. Solomon; the other, a more formal portrait, is by Philip de Laszlo.

The facts of Jerome's life show a man and writer struggling, succeeding, continually changing his mètier. But certain themes in his work are repeated; certain attitudes develop. They are best examined not through a chronological progress of his published career, but through a study of the man as a humorist, an editor, a playwright, and a serious novelist.

CHAPTER 2

The Idler as Humorist

I Jerome's Early Career

JEROME shot into fame with his splendidly humorous *Three Men in a Boat*."[1] The words are Sir Arthur Conan Doyle's, who adds that Jerome K. Jerome had a serious side, evidenced by *The Passing of the Third Floor Back*. Jerome did owe his reputation and his success, however, to the early light books of humor. Jeromian wit and "the new humor" became terms in the late nineteenth century that were used by those who enjoyed his books and by those who scorned them. By 1894 Robert Hichens, satirizing Oscar Wilde and the esthetes in his novel *The Green Carnation*, had his characters spot a philistine by his preference for the works of Jerome.

Three Men in a Boat was not, however, Jerome's first success; it climaxed a growing appreciation begun with *On the Stage—and Off* (1885), Jerome's lively account of his three years with acting companies that played to the provinces and London's East End. The chapters had first been serialized by Aylmer Gowing, a retired actor, in *The Play* and then were collected for a book. Jerome tells of his thrill in "My First Book," an essay he wrote for *The Idler*. *On the Stage—and Off* sold fairly well; "but," says Jerome, "the critics were shocked. The majority denounced it as rubbish and, three years later, on reviewing my next book, 'The Idle Thoughts of an Idle Fellow,' regretted that an author who had written such an excellent first book should have followed it up by so unworthy a successor."[2]

The second humorous book, *The Idle Thoughts of an Idle Fellow* (1889), had been previously serialized in *Home Chimes*, a magazine edited by F. W. Robinson; and some of its famous contributors were James M. Barrie, Algernon Swinburne, Coventry Patmore, Bret Harte, and Philip Mars-

ton. Jerome also wrote a feature "The Gossip's Corner" for
this magazine. On a bet with J. M. Barrie that *The Times*
would not print a letter to the editor about any shocking subject, Jerome sent one on the subject of nudity in art. The paper
did print it, followed by enough other Jerome items that
The Times in an editorial referred to him as a humorist.[3]
When *Three Men in a Boat* appeared in book form in 1889,
Jerome was sure of a public.

These books were followed by *Stage-Land* (1890), *Told
After Supper* (1891), and *Diary of a Pilgrimage* (1891).
Then Jerome stepped into the editorship of *The Idler* and
To-day, from which position he contributed features which
he later collected and reprinted as separate volumes. The six
volumes, published before Jerome assumed editorial positions, established his reputation and made him a likely choice
for an editor's chair. The homogeneity in their contents permits grouping them under three general classifications which
help in deciding what is meant by "Jeromian" or the "new
humor." Two of the books describe the theater of the times;
two recount travel experiences; two are miscellaneous humor and ghost stories.

II   On the Stage—and Off *(1885)*

On the Stage—and Off combines pathos and humor. Much
of the humor comes not from the conscious effort to be funny
but from descriptions of the second-rate theater at a time
when even English first-rate theater was deplorably bad—a
time described often as rich in actors but poor in drama. The
basic comic ingredient of the book is simply the way the
theater was, and Jerome's knowledge stems from his own
experience. The book is, therefore, autobiographical; and in
it Jerome recounts in first person "The Brief Career of a
Would-be Actor," the sub-title. The opening sentences set
the tone: "There comes a time in every one's life when he
feels he was born to be an actor. Something within him tells
him that he is the coming man. . . . He burns with a desire
to show them how the thing's done. . . . This sort of thing
generally takes a man when he is about nineteen, and lasts
tell he is nearly twenty. . . ."[4] With no less enthusiasm, the
narrator establishes a course of reading—the complete works

of Shakespeare, Jonson, Beaumont and Fletcher, Sheridan, Goldsmith, Lord Lytton. A bit discouraged after this exposure, he comes upon a book on "making-up," and the fever revives. He explores the possibilities of getting an actual playing part: the direct approach, agents, professors. For a small premium, a former manager wrangles a position for him in a Surrey-side theater where he is to serve the first month gratis, after which he will receive a "salary according to ability." The offer seems to him eminently fair. The part consists of three lines in a crowd scene, but he is not dismayed:

I did not walk back to my lodgings, I skipped back. I burst open the door, and went up the stairs like a whirlwind; but I was too excited to stop indoors. I went and had a dinner at a first-class restaurant, the bill for which considerably lessened my slender means. "Never mind," I thought, "what are a few shillings, when I shall soon be earning my hundreds of pounds!" I went to the theater, but I don't know what theater it was, or what was the play, and I don't think I knew at the time. I did notice the acting a little, but only to fancy how much better I could play each part myself. . . . Then I went home to bed, and lay awake all night, dreaming. (20–21)

Jerome next describes backstage areas of the theater, the disappointing reality of the seedy actors, and his first rehearsal. But he first makes it clear that his book describes only a small part of the theatrical world: "My short career was passed among the minor London theaters, and second and third rate traveling companies; and it is of these, and these only, that I shall speak. But of these—of what came under my actual observation, that is—I shall speak freely, endeavoring to record things exactly as I found them—nothing extenuating, nor setting down aught in malice" (26). Of the West End theater he does not speak; he has said that the West End, to those without money or influence, lay behind a closed door.[5] Of his first performance he writes:

We had five rehearsals for this play. "What the dickens do they want with so many?" was the indignant comment of the First Old Woman. "Why, they'll rehearse it more times than they'll play it." I thought five a ridiculously small number at the time . . . but there came a time when I looked upon two as betokening extraordinary anxiety about a production. In the provinces, I have known a three act comedy put on without any rehearsal at all, and with half the people not even knowing the patter. "Business" was arranged in whispered consultations, while the play was proceeding, and when things got into a more than usually glorious muddle, one or other of the characters would come off the stage and have a look at the book. (57)

Jerome describes all, scenery and supers. The stage carpenter of the London company appears to be a veritable tyrant when he insists that one cabin set will do for several interiors. The audience, which recognizes the refurbishment,

greeted its second appearance with cries of kindly recognition, and at once entered into the humor of the thing. A Surrey-side Saturday-night audience is generally inclined to be cheerful, and, if the fun on the stage doesn't satisfy them, they rely on their own resources. After one or two more appearances, the cottage became an established favorite with the gallery. So much so, indeed, that when two scenes passed without it being let down, there were many and anxious inquiries after it, and an earnest hope expressed that nothing serious had happened to it. Its reappearance in the next act (as something entirely new) was greeted with a round of applause, and a triumphant demand to know, "Who said it was lost?" (59–60)

Costuming, particularly the expense of it, to the poorly paid actor proves to be a problem; but Jerome shops about, and his sisters sew to help outfit him. First-night appearances threaten danger in that a few friends—medical students and clergymen's sons—intend to come down in a body to give him a fair start. He foils them by suggesting ahead of time that he will be appearing as an old man:

So far as I was concerned, the plan was a glorious success, but the effect upon the old man was remarkable. He was too deaf to hear exactly what was going on, but he gathered enough to be aware that he was the object of a certain amount of attention. . . . The dear fellows gave him a splendid reception when he first appeared. They applauded everything he said or did throughout the play, and called for him after every act. They encored his defiance of the villain, and, when he came on without his hat in a snow

scene, they all pulled out their pocket handkerchiefs and sobbed
aloud. At the end they sent a message round to tell him to hurry up,
as they were waiting for him at the stage door, an announcement
that had the effect of sending him out by the front way in wonder-
fully quick time. (79)

His company finishes its London run, and he joins a traveling troupe: "I only answered one advertisement, and was
engaged at once; but this, no doubt, was owing to my having
taken the precaution, when applying, of enclosing my photograph" (96). In order to contain all his costumes for going
on the road, he buys an enormous traveling basket, which
becomes an object of exasperation:

I did get a big one. I've got it now. It's downstairs in the wash
house. I've never been able to get rid of it from that day to this. I've
tried leaving it behind when removing into new lodgings, but it has
always been sent on after me, generally in a wagon with a couple
of men, who, evidently imagining they were restoring me a treasured
heirloom, have been disappointed at my complete absence of enthusiasm. I have lured stray boys into the house, and offered them
half a crown to take it away and lose it, but they have become frightened, and gone home and told their mothers, and after that, it has
got about in the neighborhood that I have committed a murder. It
isn't the sort of thing you can take out with you on a dark night, and
drop down somebody else's area. (98)

At this point in the book, Jerome recounts some of his provincial experiences in letters to a friend, Jim. By now he is
playing almost any part, though he calls himself a "Responsible" when he applies for a position. Members of the company come and go, with little incidents of jealousy, grief,
sacrifice noted. The story of "Mad Mat" gets a separate
chapter. Jerome comments on boarding houses, having, on
the whole, only kind words for landladies, though he suffers
in the process of hunting lodgings.
His next experience is with a stock company, a provincial
group that plays regularly a half a dozen towns on a regular
circuit. He finds it dull in a country town for six months at a
stretch, though the plays are better, the work is easier, and
he has an opportunity to see what the art of acting might be

when a real London star plays with them for a time. In writing
to Jim, he says:

We had crowded houses all the time he was with us, and I'm not
surprised. It must have been a treat to these benighted provincials
to see real acting. No wonder country people don't care much for
theaters, seeing the wretched horse-play presented to them under
the name of acting. It does exasperate me to hear people talking all
that thundering nonsense about the provinces being such a splendid school for young actors. Why, a couple of months of it is enough
to kill any idea of acting a man may have started with. . . .
But _____ changed all that for us. He infused a new spirit into
everybody, and, when he was on the stage, the others acted better
than I should ever have thought they could have done. . . . I
could myself tell that I was acting very differently to the way in
which I usually act. I seemed to catch his energy and his earnest-
ness; the scene grew almost real, and I began to *feel* my part.
And that is the most any one can do on the stage. (143-44)

For his next venture in his acting career, he joins a "Fitup," a traveling troupe that carries its own props and scenery
to fit up a stage in any hall, barn, or room available for hire;
the pay is uncertain, the actors poor. The East End London
theater provides a last experience, a fortnight's engagement
in which he is "guyed" in a melodrama, where his outrageous
costume produces from the audience:

"What is it, Bill?" And then another voice added: "Tell us what it
is, and you shall have it."
A good deal of laughter followed these speeches. I got hot all
over, and felt exceedingly uncomfortable and nervous. It was as
much as I could do to recollect my part, and it was with a great
effort that I began my first line. No sooner had I opened my mouth,
however, than somebody in the pit exclaimed, in tones of the utmost
surprise, "Blowed if it ain't alive!" . . . while one good-natured
man sought to put me at my ease by roaring out in a stentorian voice,
"Never you mind, old man; you go on. They're jealous 'cos you've
got nice clothes on!" How I managed to get through the part I
don't know. (159-160)

Hard times, though, have come upon England, and trade
is bad for all amusements. Managers abscond without pay-

ing, and Jerome becomes a frequent visitor to pawn shops.
One last deception by a fast-talking manager leaves the company stranded at the end of a first week's engagement:

I went back to the dressing-room, gathered my things into a bundle, and came down again with it. The others were standing about
the stage, talking low, with a weary, listless air. I passed through
them without a word, and reached the stage door. . . . I pulled
it open, and held it back with my foot, while I stood there on the
threshold for a moment, looking out at the night. Then I turned my
coat collar up, and stepped into the street: the stage door closed behind me with a bang and a click, and I have never opened another
one since. (169–70)

This passage concludes Jerome's first book, *On the Stage —
and Off*, which, in some respects, is not surpassed by his
later, better-known works. The book is short, 170 pages; and
the humor is not belabored. He writes with a happy mixture
of brashness and pity combined with honest observation.

In *My Life and Times* he records the provenience of *On
the Stage—And Off*. He had been writing romantic stories of
medieval knights and fairies, and not selling them. "It came
to me. . . not to bother about other people's trouble . . .
but to write about my own. I would tell the world the story of
a hero called Jerome who had run away and gone upon the
stage; and of all the strange and moving things that happened to him there" (69). Indeed, Jerome does capture the
"sense of strange and moving things." The discipline which
he applied to the writing of this book was a double one. First,
he had it checked for accuracy:

I hunted up an old actor named Johnson—the oldest actor on
the boards, he boasted himself. . . . He had played with Edmund
Kean, Macready, Phelps and Booth, not to mention myself. We had
been at Astley's together, during the run of *Mazeppa*. It had
fallen to our lot, in the third act, to unbind Lisa Weber from the ex-
hausted steed, and carry her across the stage. I took her head and
old Johnson her heels. She was what Mr. Mantalini would have
called a demmed fine woman. . . . I used to wait for him at the
stage door, and we would adjourn to a little tavern in Oxford
Market. . . . He would look over my MS. to see that I had made
no blunders.

Second, Jerome tried his work out on a limited public:

For a workroom I often preferred the dark streets to my dismal
bed-sitting-room. Portland Place was my favorite study. . . . I
would pause beneath each lamp-post and jot down the sentence I
had just thought out. At first the police were suspicious. I had to
explain to them. Later they got friendly; and often I would read to
them some passage I thought interesting or amusing. There was an
Inspector—a dry old Scotchman who always reached Langham
church as the clock struck eleven: he was the most difficult. When-
ever I made him laugh, I went home feeling I had done good
work.[6]

Jerome, excited about the book, finished it after working-
hours in three months. The freshness comes through to the
reader.

The interest of the book is twofold. First, the narrative of
a young man making his entry into the working world appeals. Second, the world of the theater is perennially interesting, and that of traveling troupes even more so. To Jerome's public was added a sense of nostalgia for the theater
many had known, the theater of the 1870's in the provinces
and in the suburbs. Jerome's experiences cover three or four
types of companies—the popular theater in London, those
numerous houses that played to the middle and lower classes
in the suburbs and London's East End; the touring and provincial stock companies; and the "Fitup," which Jerome calls
"only one grade higher than a booth."

Not only did the book provide contemporaries with an inside look at the popular theater, but it provides today a trea-
sury of information on the working-class drama for the enthu-
siast trying to clear the muddy picture of nineteenth-century
drama between Sheridan and Shaw. Plays named by Jerome
in which he performed, besides Shakespeare freely rendered,
include Watts Phillips' *Lost in London*, and the anonymous plays *Whittington and His Cat*, *The Honeymoon*,
The Idiot Witness, and frequently mentioned but unnamed
pantomimes. He was expected to do the hornpipe and to be
able to ad lib on "burning local questions." An evening's
performance in the provinces might include tragedy, melo-

drama, and burlesque. With one company a pantomime always preceded the tragedy.

The book contains a wealth of information seen through the eyes of an eager young man. He is at first curious and excited over what is backstage, learning how scenery is painted, how props are made, what the procedures are—what the layman does not know. Gradually, his disillusionment sets in as he discovers no dress rehearsals, no Green Room, often no dressing room, and sometimes no pay. But the tone is never bitter, never unkind.

The humor turns mostly on the knack of deflating himself, as in the opening sentences of the book (quoted above); upon making a situation ridiculous by exaggeration, as in the case of the wicker basket; or, the feature he was to develop in his *Idle Thoughts*, the shared exasperation—for example, "They charged me extra for the basket on the Great Eastern Line, and I have hated that company ever since" (116).

Jerome's narrative style is that of the familiar essay, even the familiar letter, colloquial and friendly. He relates conversation in standard English or in Cockney with good effect and with ease. The structure is loose, and the device of writing letters to Jim seems a makeshift. The chapter on "Mad Mat" forms a kind of character sketch, with too little motivation for either the madness or the death for the piece to be called a short story. The conclusion to the chapter "'Mad Mat' Has an Opportunity" strikes the somber note that occurs occasionally as Jerome keeps the reader aware of the sordid side of stage life: "I never expected to see Mat again, and I never did. People who have lived for any length of time on six shillings a week don't take long to die when they set about it, and two days after I had seen him, Mad Mat's opportunity came, and he took it" (115).

The book is not a novel, and no characters other than the narrator are given more than temporary attention. By the end of the book the narrator has achieved a clear personality. Others are briefly but clearly sketched, and they are in some ways better than the characters from this same theatrical experience that Jerome uses in his autobiographical novel *Paul Kelver*, where he gives the reader Mrs. Peebles and the O'Kelleys from his barnstorming days.

In summary, *On the Stage—and Off* provides good humorous reading and authentic information for an increasingly interesting phase of the nineteenth-century drama.

III   Stage-Land *(1890)*

Stage-Land, Curious Habits and Customs of its Inhabitants, described by Jerome K. Jerome and illustrated by Bernard Partridge, is Jerome's second humorous book on the theater. "The book was quite a success," Jerome writes in *My Life and Times*. "They were the palmy days of the old Adelphi. Sims and Pettitt, Manville Fenn, Augustus Harris, Arthur Shirley, Dion Boucicault and H. A. Jones were all writing melodrama" (84). While the book stems from Jerome's personal experience in the theatrical world, the approach differs from *On the Stage—and Off*. *Stage-Land* comprises fourteen short chapters about the stereotypes of melodrama. Jerome's own summary from *My Life and Times* best condenses the book:

The Stage Hero, his chief aim in life to get himself accused of crimes he had never committed; the Villain, the only man in the play possessed of a dress suit; the Heroine, always in trouble; the Stage Lawyer, very old and very long and very thin; the Adventuress, with a habit of mislaying her husbands; the Stage Irishman, who always paid his rent and was devoted to his landlord; the Stage Sailor, whose trousers never fitted him—they were well-known characters. All now are gone. If Partridge and myself helped to hasten their end, 1 am sorry. They were better—more human, more understandable—than many of the new puppets that have taken their place. (84)

The tone of the entire book is tongue-in-cheek satire—the innocent refusal to divorce stage life from reality. Bernard Partridge's first sketch shows a cockney in a bowler hat at the balcony edge surrounded by a dedication: "To that highly respectable but unnecessarily retiring individual of whom we hear so much but see so little, 'The earnest student of the drama,' this (comparatively) truthful little book is lovingly dedicated."[7]

Each essay makes the naive assumption that all stage life is true. For example, of the stage heroine he writes:

Nothing goes right with her. We all have our troubles, but the Stage heroine never has anything else. If she only got one afternoon a week off from trouble, or had her Sundays free, it would be something.

But no! misfortune stalks beside her from week's beginning to week's end.

After her husband has been found guilty of murder . . . and her white-haired father has become a bankrupt, and has died of a broken heart, and the home of her childhood has been sold up, then her infant goes and contracts a lingering fever. . . . Her excessive goodness seems somehow to pall upon us. Our only consolation, while watching her, is that there are not many good women off the stage. (35–37)

Then she has difficulty with the snow: "The stage heroine's only pleasure in life is to go out in a snowstorm without an umbrella, and with no bonnet on. . . . Maybe she fears the snow will spoil it, and she is a careful girl. She always brings her child out with her on these excursions. She seems to think that it will freshen it up. . . . One thing that must irritate the Stage heroine very much, on these occasions, is the way in which the snow seems to lie in wait for her, and follow her about" (38).

The Stage child seems to Jerome particularly obnoxious: "It is nice and quiet and it talks pretty. We have come across real infants, now and then, in the course of visits to married friends; they have been brought to us from outlying parts of the house, and introduced to us for our edification; and we have found them gritty and sticky. . . . And they have talked to us—but not pretty, not at all—rather rude we should call it. But the Stage child is very different. It is clean and tidy. You can touch it anywhere and nothing comes off."(97)

The chapter on the Stage peasants begins:[5]

They are so clean. We have seen peasantry off the stage, and it has presented an untidy—occasionally a disreputable and unwashed appearance; but the Stage peasant seems to spend all his wages on soap and hair oil. . . .

They are so happy. They don't look it, but we know they are, because they say so. If you don't believe them, they dance three steps
to the right and three steps to the left back again. They can't help
it. It is because they are so happy. . . . What particularly rouses
them is the heroine's love affairs. They could listen to that all day.

They yearn to hear what she said to him. . . . In our own love-
sick days, we often used to go and relate to various people all the
touching conversations that took place between *our* lady-love
and ourselves; but *our* friends never seemed to get excited over
it. . . . They had trains to catch, and men to meet, before we had
got a quarter through the job. (124–25)

A last quotation will illustrate tone and style. This passage
is from "The Good Old Man": "He has lost his wife. But he
knows where she is—among the angels! She isn't all gone,
because the heroine has her hair. . . . The people on the
stage think very highly of the good old man, but they don't
encourage him much, after the first act. He generally dies
in the first act. If he does not seem likely to die, they murder
him" (133).

The essays, set pieces, are amusing when not carried on
too long. The later ones on minor characters are shorter and
relatively better. Presented as they first were in serial form,
they could well have been a delightful feature of Heneage
Mandell's *The Playgoer*, a magazine which was an out-
growth of the Playgoers' Club, of which Jerome was an orga-
nizer. Jerome contributed the original sketches unsigned,
and "journals that had been denouncing me and all my work
as an insult to English literature hastened to crib them."[8]
For the book edition, Bernard Partridge, an illustrator for
Punch, drew the sketches, and Jerome and Partridge published the book themselves, profitably. Partridge drew himself for "The Hero," and Gertrude Kingston, the actress, sat
for "The Adventuress." Like *"On the Stage—and Off, Stage-
Land* has become a source book, truly, for the modern
"earnest student of the drama."[9]

IV   Three Men in a Boat *(1889)*

The most popular of Jerome's work, *Three Men in a Boat—
To Say Nothing of the Dog,* began as a serious travel book—
descriptions of the Thames with bits of history and humorous

relief. He succeeded in writing the "slabs of history"; but
F. W. Robinson, who was publishing the book serially in
Home Chimes, rejected them. Halfway through, Jerome
changed the idea and the title and quickly finished the
book. The preface to the first edition reads:

> The chief beauty of this book lies not so much in its literary style,
> or in the extent and usefulness of the information it conveys, as in
> its simple truthfulness. Its pages form the record of events that
> really happened. All that has been done is to colour them; and, for
> this, no extra charge has been made. George and Harris and Mont-
> morency are not poetic ideals, but things of flesh and blood—espe-
> cially George, who weighs about twelve stone. Other works may
> excel this in depth of thought and knowledge of human nature:
> other books may rival it in originality and size; but, for hopeless
> and incurable veracity, nothing yet discovered can surpass it. This,
> more than all its other charms, will, it is felt, make the volume pre-
> cious in the eye of the earnest reader; and will lend additional
> weight to the lesson that the story teaches.[10]

George, Harris, and "I," who was Jerome, were real.
Harris was Carl Hentschel, a young man working with his
father on photo-etching, a process that enabled newspapers
to print pictures. George was George Wingrave, who became
a bank manager. He and Jerome had shared lodgings when
both were beginning their careers. "There wasn't any dog.
I did not possess a dog in those days. . . . Montmorency
I evolved out of my inner consciousness. There is something
of the dog, I take it, in most Englishmen."[11] There is something of the boating adventurer, too, in most people; and so
long as camping out and boating remain popular, *Three Men
in a Boat* will probably be enjoyed. Like Robinson Crusoe's
experience, this adventure seems to belong to Everyman.

The three men had often gone boating on Sunday morn-
ings, taking the train to Richmond, carrying their picnic
hampers, and wearing fancy blazers. "I did not have to
imagine or invent. Boating up and down the Thames had
been a favourite sport ever since I could afford it. I just put
down the things that happened."[12] It is not quite that simple,
but the art of making everyday incidents a source of shared

amusement, seemingly without effort, is Jerome's forte. The book begins:

There were four of us—George, and William Samuel Harris, and myself, and Montmorency. We were sitting in my room, smoking, and talking about how bad we were—bad from a medical point of view I mean, of course.

We were all feeling seedy, and we were getting quite nervous about it. Harris said he felt such extraordinary fits of giddiness come over him at times, that he hardly knew what he was doing; and then George said that *he* had fits of giddiness too, and hardly knew what *he* was doing. With me, it was my liver that was out of order, because I had just been reading a patent liver-pill circular, in which were detailed the various symptoms by which a man could tell when his liver was out of order. I had them all. (3)

After discussing their complaints and rambling upon remedies, they hit upon the plan of a week on the river from Kingston to Oxford and back.

Preparations demand a great amount of discussion—what food to take, what kind of tent, or should they overnight at inns? Harris says: "'Now, the first thing to settle is what to take with us. Now, you get a bit of paper and write down, J., and you get the grocery catalogue, George, and somebody give me a bit of pencil, and then I'll make out a list.' That's Harris all over—so ready to take the burden of everything himself, and put it on the backs of other people. He always reminds me of my poor Uncle Podger" (19). And he then turns to the story of Uncle Podger and picture-hanging, happily accompanied by one of A. Frederics' sketches.

The subject of clothes comes next: "George said two suits of flannel would be sufficient as we could wash them ourselves, in the river, when they got dirty. We asked him if he had ever tried washing flannels in the river, and he replied; 'No, not exactly himself like; but he knew some fellows who had, and it was easy enough'; and Harris and I were weak enough to fancy he knew what he was talking about, and that three respectable young men, without position or influence, and with no experience in washing, could really clean their own shirts and trousers in the River Thames with a bit of soap"(26).

Packing has to be done, and everyone contributes his criticism. When all is ready, Harris and Jerome bring everything to the doorstep to load into a cab, which, of course, is not forthcoming:

It did look a lot, and Harris and I began to feel rather ashamed of it. . . . No cab came by, but the street boys did, and got interested in the show, apparently, and stopped. . . . Bigg's boy . . . came round the corner. . . . In another moment, the grocer's boy came across, and took up a position on the other side of the step. Then the young gentleman from the boot-shop stopped. . . . "They ain't a-going to starve, are they?" said the gentleman from the boot-shop. "Ah! you'd want to take a thing or two with *you*, retorted The Blue Posts, "if you was a-going to cross the Atlantic in a small boat." "They ain't a-going to cross the Atlantic," struck in Bigg's boy, "they're a-going to find Stanley" (42–43).

The trip up the river is full of difficulties of rowing, upsetting the teakettle, forgetting the tin-opener, and getting lost in the Hampton Court maze. Jerome learns a bit about rowing up stream, and considers the scenery as well:

We reached Sunbury lock at half past three. The river is sweetly pretty just there before you come to the gates, and the backwater is charming; but don't attempt to row up it. I tried to do so once. . . . I pulled splendidly. I got well into a steady rhythmical swing. I put my arms and legs and my back into it. I set myself a good, quick, dashing stroke, and worked in really grand style. My two friends said it was a pleasure to watch me. At the end of five minutes . . . we were under the bridge, in exactly the same spot that we were when I began, and there were those two idiots, injuring themselves by violent laughing. (72)

They have difficulty with a tow line, with the locks, and occasionally with another boat:

I don't know why it should be, but everybody is always so exceptionally irritable on the river. Little mishaps, that you would hardly notice on dry land, drive you nearly frantic with rage, when they occur on the water. When Harris or George makes an ass of himself on dry land, I smile indulgently; but when they behave in a chuckle-headed way on the river, I use the most blood-curdling language

to them. . . . The air of the river has a demoralizing effect upon
one's temper, and this it is, I suppose, which causes even bargemen
to be sometimes rude to one another, and to use language which,
no doubt, in their calmer moments they regret. (168–69)

The outing ends, as one might predict, with their giving
up a day early when the rains come and taking the train back
to London:

Then Harris, who was sitting next to the window, drew aside the
curtain and looked out upon the street.

It glistened darkly in the wet, the dim lamps flickered with each
gust, the rain splashed steadily into the puddles and trickled down
the water-spouts into the running gutters. A few soaked wayfarers
hurried past, crouching beneath their dripping umbrellas, the wom-
en holding up their skirts.

"Well," said Harris, reaching his hand out for his glass, "We have
had a pleasant trip, and my hearty thanks for it to old Father
Thames—but we did well to chuck it when we did. Here's to
Three Men well out of a Boat!"

And Montmorency, standing on his hind legs, before the window, peering out into the night, gave a short bark of decided con-
currence with the toast. (178)

These passages represent the book. Almost any page would
yield anecdote, homely reflection, young man-about-town
slang, and innocent ragging.

It is a sobering process to analyze humor; and, on the
whole, criticism must give way to simple appreciation.
Jerome was always quick to recognize that what seems funny depends often upon time and the mood. He need not
have been so offended with the criticism of *Punch*, for
example. The Baron de Bookworm, admittedly ill when he
read it, finds that it does not tickle his risibilities as does
Pickwick. The Baron, however, does compliment Jerome's
Stage-Land, and he admits that other young critics find
Three Men in a Boat immensely amusing but nothing to
laugh at in *Pickwick*. His chief complaint seems to be that
Jerome's humor weakly imitates American fun and uses a
low sort of slang. It appears an odd criticism when examined amid the surrounding pages of *Punch*, full of what

to the modern reader looks very like the same type of humor. Nevertheless, "new humor" became the term of opprobrium hurled at Jerome by more sophisticated writers, a term later extended to include members of his staff on *The Idler* and *To-day*.

Jerome's humor in *Three Men in a Boat* consists first of all in the basic ability to make a good story out of the most trivial of incidents. He is a raconteur who can tell funny stories. The laugh comes either because he turns the joke on himself—his embarrassments, his mistakes, even his conceit—or because he gives an unexpected twist to the climax of an incident or even a sentence. V. S. Pritchett, in his review of the book upon its reprint in 1957, says that the laughter in Jerome is caused less by any fact than by the false conclusions drawn from it; and he refers to the passage quoted above about swearing on the river. To Pritchett, "Skilfully Jerome plays everything down. He relies on misleading moral commentary and on that understatement which runs like a rheumatism through English humor."[13]

Like most humorists, Jerome depends on exaggeration and understatement. He may make the reality absurd or, inversely, treat absurdity with gravity. There is nothing new about these characteristics, but what succeeded at the time as something fresh with a large public was just that touch of brashness in treating ordinary subjects.

Professor Donald Gray, in "The Uses of Victorian Laughter," speaks of one of the uses of laughter as "to furnish a holiday from taking things and ideas seriously," the laughter of release.[14] Such is the principal quality of the fun in *Three Men in a Boat*. It is not so much that the situations are ridiculous or exaggerated but that they are familiar to anyone's experience. *Three Men in a Boat* does provide chuckles at the foibles of mankind, and it creates a genial pleasure in an imagined trip up the river. George, Harris, and Jerome seem scarcely distinguishable despite their colorful comments about one another. They do not strike the modern reader, however, as quite as "low" as the *Punch* critic found them.

In England, in America, where pirated copies ran to the millions, and in dozens of translations *Three Men in a Boat* has become a classic of humor. Of all Jerome's books it is the most easily available and perhaps the most appreciated.

V   Diary of a Pilgrimage *(1890)*

Diary of a Pilgrimage records Jerome's first trip to Germany. He had wanted to see the Passion Play at Oberammergau, so with Walter Helmore, a young insurance agent, as companion, he set off on a trip. These were the days when Germany and England were feeling their kinship; but, because the tourist business had not developed to any great degree, travelers lodged with peasants and shared their fare.

In the first-person narrative Jerome begins by accepting the invitation to travel to Germany, for he is as much interested in the trip as in the play. As he fancies himself a world traveler, he concocts in his mind the suavity and savoir-faire with which he will recount his travels. His companion deflates him with a spoof on the travel book by using the sights of London instead of far-off countries. Inevitably, a chapter on packing for the trip follows, and an inevitable comic description of a Channel crossing in rough weather is included. With these perennial subjects for laughter, Jerome amuses, and he is abetted by frequent, clever sketches by G. G. Fraser.

Jerome keeps loosely to the form of a diary as he records his first impressions of traveling abroad. He amuses with the subjects of German beds, the inconveniences of the small inn, and particularly foreign languages and foreign-language phrase books: "At the end of the book were German proverbs and 'Idiomatic Phrases,' . . . 'One should not buy a cat in a sack,'—as if there were a large class of consumers who habitually did purchase their cats in that way, thus enabling unscrupulous dealers to palm off upon them an inferior cat, and whom it was accordingly necessary to advise against the custom."[15]

The performance of the Passion Play has to be treated seriously. He introduces this subject by asking his companion what can possibly be written about a topic so well known. The companion hands back what amounts to program notes on the history of the performance and the village actors. Jerome's conclusions are sober, reflecting his religious beliefs:

Few believing Christians among the vast audience but must have passed out from that strange playhouse with belief and love strengthened. . . . A cultivated mind needs no story of human suffering to win or hold it to a faith. But the imaginative and the cultured are few and far between, and the peasants of Oberammergau can plead, as their Master himself once pleaded, that they seek not to help the learned but the lowly. The unbeliever, also, passes out into the village street full of food for thought. . . . Not by his doctrines . . . has Christ laid hold upon the hearts of men, but by the story of his life. (158-59)

Jerome follows this observation with a short discussion of the performers as actors; but he is happily interrupted by the disturbance next door, rising from the fact that the roomers there have to pass through Jerome's room to get to the stairway.

Jerome discusses the tourist and the travel agent. Art galleries are treated by Jerome and his friend with much the same levity as Mark Twain used, but Jerome adds, "I shall not say anything about [the old masters], as I do not wish to disturb in any way the critical opinion that Europe has already formed concerning them" (176). It does seem to them, though, that twenty-five percent of the pictures deal with foodstuffs. As for the travelers themselves, German bands and beer gardens completely delight them.

The travelers have difficulties with German timetables; German trains plague them, but their journey ends, and Jerome sums up his trip with complimentary first impressions on Germany and the Germans:

They are a simple, earnest, homely, genuine people. They do not laugh much; but when they do, they laugh deep down. . . . A visit to Germany is a tonic to an Englishman. We English are always sneering at ourselves, and patriotism in England is regarded as a stamp of vulgarity. The Germans, on the other hand, believe in themselves, and respect themselves. The world for them is not played out. Their country to them is still the "Fatherland." They look straight before them like a people who see a great future in front of them, and are not afraid to go forward to fulfill it. (212–13)

Following the material about the pilgrimage, Jerome included six essays on varied subjects, the type of essay to be found in *Idle Thoughts of an Idle Fellow*. These essays concern dreams, clocks, teakettles, a dog, the difficulties of writing a pathetic story when assigned to do so by the editor, and the sad situation of the writer who sells his integrity for success:

Thus he became rich and famous and great; and had fine clothes to wear and rich food to eat, as the demon had promised him . . . only at the bottom of his desk there lay (and he had never had the courage to destroy them) a little pile of faded manuscripts, written in a boyish hand, that would speak to him of the memory of a poor lad who had once paced the city's feet-worn stones, dreaming of no other greatness than that of being one of God's messengers to men, and who had died, and had been buried for all eternity, long years ago. (33)

The last essay, "The New Utopia," pokes fun at rich young Socialists. Jerome has a dream in which he awakens to find himself in the twenty-ninth century—a fast-moving but drab period where joy and grief alike have been leveled, marriage has been eliminated, birth is controlled, and conformity prevails. People are known by numbers and are strictly regulated by a Majority; and the Majority is their god. Any sign of genius or extraordinary physical size is lopped off by surgery or brain-softening. In a short essay, Jerome predicts an Orwellian "1984" in a decade when William Morris and Edward Bellamy are picturing Utopian futures where private gains have been eliminated for the joy of a classless state.[16]

. *Diary of a Pilgrimage* probably deserves the oblivion into which it has slipped. As travel humor, it lacks the freshness of *Three Men in a Boat;* and Jerome writes better on Germany, in *Three Men on the Bummel*. The essays, all but the last, which deserves a reprinting in some collection of Utopian essays, are fair reading.

VI   Idle Thoughts of an Idle Fellow *(1889)*

Idle Thoughts of an Idle Fellow collects fourteen essays on miscellaneous subjects which Jerome first wrote for monthly serialization in F. W. Robinson's *Home Chimes*. Jerome received a guinea apiece for the essays, but the opportunity to publish with Robinson, who was editor for such writers as Swinburne, Watts-Dunton, Dr. Westland Marston the dramatist, J. M. Barrie, and Coventry Patmore, marked an important step. Robinson "liked my essay . . . [because] there was a new note in it," Jerome recalls.[17] Mr. Tuer of the Leadenhall Press published the English book edition in an attractive, light yellow cover. Each thousand he called an edition, and soon he was advertising the twenty-third edition. When Jerome received twopence halfpenny per copy, he dreamed of a fur coat. American printings, pirated in the hundreds of thousands just a few years before the international copyright agreement, paid Jerome no royalty.

The humor of *Idle Thoughts of an Idle Fellow* is not the boisterous fun of the young men, nor the laughter of release. It is rather thoughtful laughter, based on common sense and observation; and it frequently gives rise to sober reflection by both author and reader. The subject matter roams the field of everyday experiences: "On Being Hard Up," "On Being in the Blues," "On Vanity and Vanities," "On Getting on in the World," "On Being Idle," "On Being in Love," "On the Weather," "On Cats and Dogs," "On Being Shy," "On Babies," "On Eating and Drinking," "On Furnished Apartments," "On Dress and Deportment," "On Memory."

After a dedication to his pipe, a mocking preface introduces the essays, claiming a public demand for them—that is, by his relatives, but disclaiming any elevated thought: "All I can suggest is, that when you get tired of reading 'the best hundred books,' you may take this up for half an hour. It will be a change."[18] In the first essay, "On Being Hard Up," Jerome can be both facetious and serious. He speaks from experience:

There have been a good many funny things said and written about hardupishness, but the reality is not funny, for all that. It is not funny to have to haggle over pennies. It isn't funny to be thought mean and stingy. It isn't funny to be shabby, and to be ashamed of your address. No, there is nothing at all funny in poverty—to the poor. It is hell upon earth to a sensitive man. . . . Being poor is a mere trifle. It is being known to be poor that is the sting. . . . It is easy enough to say that poverty is no crime. . . . It is a blunder though, and is punished as such. (14–15)

But, before the essay continues too long in this tone, he gives a twist through the mention of the pawnshop; and, before long, he depicts the young man's first experience at pawning:

A boy popping his first questions is confidence itself compared with him. He hangs about outside the shop, until he has succeeded in attracting the attention of all the loafers in the neighbourhood, and has aroused strong suspicions in the mind of the policeman on the beat. At last, after a careful examination of the contents of the windows, made for the purpose of impressing the by-standers with the notion that he is going in to purchase a diamond bracelet or some such trifle, he enters, trying to do so with a careless swagger, and giving himself the air of a member of the swell mob. When inside, he speaks in so low a voice as to be perfectly inaudible, and has to say it all over again. (17)

Jerome gives the essay a neat turn at the end by requesting the reader for a needed five pounds. The whole scene is the kind which Robert Benchley, in the 1930's and 1940's developed into delightful movie skits.

"On Being in the Blues" illustrates Jerome's ability to catch the characteristic speech of different people:

The symptons of the infirmity are much the same in every case, but the affliction itself is variously termed. The poet says that "a feeling of sadness comes o'er him." 'Arry refers to the heavings of his wayward heart by confiding to Jimee that he has "got the blooming hump." Your sister doesn't know what is the matter with her to-night. She feels out of sorts altogether, and hopes nothing is going to happen. The everyday-young-man is "so awfully glad to meet you, old fellow," for he does "feel so jolly miserable, this evening." As for myself, I generally say that "I have a strange, unsettled feeling to-night," and "think I'll go out."

By the way, it never does come except in the evening. (25–26)

The homely reflection follows: "But, as a rule, it is not trouble that makes us melancholy. The actuality is too stern a thing for sentiment. . . . There is no pathos in real misery: no luxury in real grief" (27).

"On Being Idle," placed centrally in the book, connects the essays to the title. His thesis about idling is that "it is impossible to enjoy idling thoroughly unless one has plenty of work to do"(61). In fact, he claims special skill as an idler: "Now this is a subject on which I flatter myself I really am *au fait*. . . . Idling has always been my strong point. I take no credit to myself in the matter—it is a gift. Few possess it. There are plenty of lazy people and plenty of slow-coaches, but a genuine idler is a rarity. He is not a man who slouches about with his hands in his pockets. On the contrary, his most startling characteristic is that he is always intensely busy" (61–61).

Such statements allow for the anecdotes to follow, purportedly about his own experiences. The exuberance with which he returns to the city after idling in a resort reveals Jerome's love for London: "But the days still passed slowly . . . and I was heartily glad when the last one came, and I was being whirled away from gouty, consumptive Buxton to London with its stern work and life. I looked out of the carriage as we rushed through Hendon in the evening. The lurid glare overhanging the mighty city seemed to warm my heart, and, when later on, my cab rattled out of St. Pancras' station, the old familiar roar that came swelling up around me sounded the sweetest music I had heard for many a long day" (66–67).

The next essay, "On Being in Love," written just a short time before Jerome married, establishes his belief that genuine love comes but once and that it differs distinctly from affection: "No, we never sicken with love twice. Cupid spends no second arrow on the same heart. Love's handmaids are our life-long friends. Respect, and Admiration, and Affection, our doors may always be left open for, but their great celestial master, in his royal progress, pays but one visit, and departs. We like, we cherish, we are very, very fond of—but we never love again. . . . Love is too pure a light to burn long among the noisome gases that we breathe, but before it is choked out we may use it as a torch to ignite the cosy fire of affection" (74–75). Jerome addresses an imaginary lecture to Edwin and Angelina: "I am afraid, dear Edwin and Angelina, you expect too much from love. You think there is enough of your little hearts to feed this fierce, devouring passion for all your long lives. Ah, young folks! don't rely too much upon that unsteady flicker. . . . You will watch it die out in anger and disappointment" (76). Jerome virtually repeats this statement to his fictional daughter and son in *They and I*, and the theme of dual love Jerome uses repeatedly in his works.

In "On the Weather" he again declares his allegiance to the city and condemns changing weather to the country where it may be suitable: "Weather in towns is like a skylark in a country-house—out of place, and in the way. Towns ought to be covered in, warmed by hot water pipes, and lighted by electricity. The weather is a country lass, and does not appear to advantage in town. We like well enough to flirt with her in the hay field, but she does not seem so fascinating when we meet her in Pall Mall. There is too much of her there" (94).

On the subject of "Cats and Dogs" Jerome could be sure of a favorable reaction. "Cats have the credit of being more worldly wise than dogs—of looking more after their own interests, and being less blindly devoted to those of their friends. And we men and women are naturally shocked at such selfishness. Cats certainly do love a family that has a carpet in the kitchen more than a family that has not; and if there are many children about, they prefer to spend their leisure time next door. But, taken altogether, cats are libelled" (115).

After cats, Jerome discusses rats; and on mention of the Pied Piper of Hamelin, he uses the metaphor seriously in talking of death: "One day the sweet sad strains will sound out full and clear, and then we too shall, like the little children, throw our playthings all aside, and follow. The loving hands will be stretched out to stay us, and the voices we have learnt to listen for will cry to us to stop. But we shall push the fond arms gently back, and pass out through the sorrowing house and through the open door. For the wild

strange music will be ringing in our hearts, and we shall
know the meaning of its song by then" (121). Rather apolo-
getic about this sentimental passage, he lightens the tone by
the next sentence: "I wish people could love animals without getting maudlin over them, as so many do" (121).

One more passage from this essay seems appealing: "And
when we bury our face in our hands and wish we had never
been born, they [the cat or dog] don't sit up very straight,
and observe that we have brought it all upon ourselves. They
don't even hope it will be a warning to us. But they come up
softly; and shove their heads against us. If it is a cat, she
stands on your shoulder, rumples your hair and says, 'lor', I
am sorry for you, old man,' as plain as words can speak; and
if it is a dog, he looks up at you with his big, true eyes, and
says with them, 'Well, you've always got me, you know.' "
(112).

"On Being Shy" begins: "All great literary men are shy.
I am myself though I am told it is hardly noticeable" (128).
He continues: "The shy man does have some slight revenge
upon society for the torture it inflicts upon him. He is able,
to a certain extent, to communicate his misery. He frightens other people as much as they frighten him. He acts like a
damper upon the whole room, and the most jovial spirits become, in his presence, depressed and nervous" (129).

In "On Babies," Jerome the bachelor imagines no "Dream
Children":

Why do babies have such yards of unnecessary clothing? It is not a
riddle. I really want to know. I never could understand it. Is it that
the parents are ashamed of the size of the child, and wish to make
believe that it is longer than it actually is? I asked a nurse once why
it was. She said—

"Lor', sir, they always have long clothes, bless their little hearts."

And when I explained that her answer, although doing credit to
her feelings, hardly disposed of my difficulty, she replied—

"Lor', sir, you wouldn't have 'em in *short* clothes, poor little
dears?" And she said it in a tone that seemed to imply I had suggested some unmanly outrage. (143)

In the essay "Eating and Drinking," which, on the whole
is light in tone, he includes at the end a sudden strident defense of drinking among the poor:

But think, before you hold up your hands in horror at their ill-living, what "life" for these wretched creatures really means. Picture the squalid misery of their brutish existence, dragged on from year to year in the narrow noisome room where, huddled like vermin in sewers, they welter, and sicken, and sleep; where dirt-grimed children scream and fight, and sluttish, shrill-voiced women cuff, and curse, and nag; where the street outside teems with roaring filth, and the house around is a bedlam of riot and stench. . . . From the hour when they crawl from their comfortless bed to the hour when they lounge back into it again, they never live one moment of real life. . . . In the name of the God of mercy let them pour the maddening liquor down their throats, and feel for one brief moment that they live! (171–73)

"Furnished Apartments" provides a description of furniture likely to be found in lodgings: "There must surely be some secret manufactory for the production of lodging-house ornaments. Precisely the same articles are to be found at every lodging-house all over the kingdom, and *they are never seen anywhere else*" (180-81). After detailing some of the miseries of living on the third-floor back or in an attic room, he concludes: "It is a long time ago, now, that I last saw the inside of an attic. I have tried various floors since, but I have not found that they have made much difference to me. Life tastes much the same, whether we quaff it from a golden goblet, or drink it out of a stone mug. . . . When we reside in an attic, we enjoy a supper of fried fish and stout. When we occupy the first floor, it takes an elaborate dinner at the 'Continental' to give us the same amount of satisfaction"(190).

A comment on Uriah Heep, in "On Dress and Deportment," will find most readers agreeing: "A meek deportment is a great mistake in this world. Uriah Heep's father was a very poor judge of human nature, or he would not have told his son, as he did, that people liked humbleness. There is nothing annoys them more, as a rule. Rows are half the fun of life, and you can't have rows with humble, meek-hearted individuals. They turn away our wrath, and that is just what we do not want" (203).

The book ends with an essay on memory, which introduces the subject of ghosts—here only the ghosts of memory; but Jerome later becomes much interested, as an Idler, in telling ghost stories. He concludes the essay with the

ghost of himself as a boy, going through the several ages of
man until boy and self, the writer, merge. It is a familiar
pattern but not the less pleasant reading and makes a suitable ending to the book.

Sentiment and laughter continually contrast and converge
in the essays, for Jerome believed that the two moods were
the stuff of human life. His cynicism is light, very light—more
a lament that the glow of idealism dims than a feeling of
bitterness or scorn toward life's ironies. Only when he
reflects on the poor, the really destitute, does he become
severe. The subjects of his essays are not controversial; continuing in the tradition of "Elia," they comment genially
on familiar universals.

His style is casual. He makes no pretenese to Augustan
polish. Characteristic, in fact, of the new humor is the conversational style of the ordinary person. Jerome uses con-
tractions plentifully and an occasional "he don't." Part of the
pleasure lies in the occasional ambiguity of colloquial
speech—for example, "I had a nephew who was once the
amateur long-distance bicycle champion. I have him still—",
or "Our next door neighbour comes out in the back garden
every now and then, and says it's doing the country a world
of good—not his coming out into the back garden, but the
weather." Some of the metaphors are fresh—for example,
the cat swears "like a medical student." Slang, dialect,
homely phrasing, such as "the curtains want washing,"
abound. He spares us the pun, that foundation of so much of
Punch humor. The essays read easily and sound like the
conversation of a good talker. Anecdotes remain brief, and
each of the essays is short.

Critics of his time labeled Jerome's style vulgar, and the
writing ungrammatical; but the public liked it. Today, the
style seems journalistic, familiar in the way of current newspaper columns. Underlying his subject matter and style is
what George Meredith in his *The Idea of Comedy* stated
in 1877 to be the truest test of comedy—that it should awak-
en thoughtful laughter and that the foundation of its appreciation should be common sense. *Idle Thoughts of an Idle
Fellow* meets the test.

In *Idle Thoughts of an Idle Fellow* Jerome established

himself firmly with a mass audience. Wisely, he retained the
cognomen of Idler, continuing to use it as an identity in
subsequent collections of essays and in his magazine title
and feature column.

VII   Told After Supper *(1891)*

Told After Supper appeared as a Christmas number,
printed on blue paper with numerous illustrations by K. M.
Skeaping—a slight book, published for the seasonal trade.
The introduction talks of ghosts at Christmastime, and Jerome
insists that it is always the guests who see the ghosts and
usually at this season; for only an occasional bourgeois ghost
appears at Hallowe'en.

This book is the first of Jerome's to use the framework device. The characters who loosely hold the stories together
are the locate curate, the doctor, a member of the County
Council, Teddy Biffles, "I," and "My Uncle." All are gathered at "My Uncle's" in Tooting after a Christmas Eve
supper of hot veal pasties, toasted lobsters, and warm
cheesecakes—all washed down by old ale and a special brew
of whisky punch. The curate begins by demonstrating some
card tricks, which do not succeed. The narrator tells a funny
story, but it seems nobody is listening. All the talkers are a
bit tipsy, so much so that the curate's story, continually interrupted, gets lost in the telling. Teddy Biffin's story of
"Johnson and Emily, or the Faithful Ghost," probably the
best story, recounts how Johnson, too poor to marry, goes to
Australia. When he comes back, the family has gone. He
dies but haunts the house, still looking for Emily. The
tenants finally decide to erect a gravestone for Emily, after
which the ghost, extremely grateful, now haunts only the
stone instead of the house.

In the uncle's story, a man who can't stand music kills a
Christmas "wait" and two cornet players; and he haunts the
house where the stories are being told. By reputation, he
comes only when bad music is heard in the blue room. The
narrator, who insists the story is true, tells of sleeping in the
blue room. While he is talking the candle falls from his hand,
and he sees a blue phantom, smoking. Ghost and narrator
have a pleasant chat. The ghost with modest pride admits

that he has killed seven—counting trombones. All were
musicians. He hates cocks, too, because they crow at the
wrong time. When they crow at this moment in the story,
the narrator walks out with the ghost. When they meet the
Constable, he seems unable to see the ghost. He even doubts
the explanation as he helps the narrator back to his uncle's
house.

All of these ghost stories are amusing ones. There is no
hint of the more serious discussion to come later in *The
Idler* magazine when the subject of ghosts arises. *Told
After Supper* must rank as one of the many Victorian Christmas specials written for the market and with no particular
literary value. Its blue paper, criticized by *Punch*, now
makes the book a more desirable collector's item.

On the strength, though, of his reputation as a humorist,
Jerome was now to enter a major phase of his literary career.
He would become the editor of two journals.

CHAPTER 3

The Idler as Editor

I   The Idler

THE period of the 1890's produced a spate of new magazines and newspapers that created exciting times for
young writers. W. T. Stead, the editor of the *Review of
Reviews*, writing in 1891 at the end of their first year of
publication, quotes Mr. John Morley's valedictory words in
leaving the *Fortnightly Review* in 1882:

The success of the reviews . . . marks a very considerable revolution in the intellectual habits of the time. They have brought
abstract discussion from the library down to the parlour, and from
the serious student to the man in the street. . . .
    The common man of the world would now listen and have
an opinion of his own on the basis of belief just as he listens
and judges in politics, or arts, or letters. The clergy no longer
have the pulpit to themselves, for the new reviews became
more powerful pulpits, in which heretics were at least as
welcome as orthodoxy.

"If this was true of the half-crown reviews," W. T. Stead
adds, "how much more true is it of the sixpenny monthly."[1]
The Idler, edited by Jerome K. Jerome and Robert Barr,
beginning in February 1892, was a sixpenny monthly.
    Robert Barr, who had made a success of the English edi-
tion of the *Detroit Free Press*, wished to start something
of his own. "He wanted a popular name," Jerome writes,
"and at first, was undecided between Kipling and myself.
He chose me—as, speaking somewhat bitterly, he later on
confessed to me—thinking that I should be the easier to
'manage.' He had not liked the look of Kipling's jaw."[2] The
idea of the magazine was Barr's, but the title was Jerome's,

who capitalized on the popularity of his own *Idle Thoughts
of an Idle Fellow* (1889).

With no formal editorial fanfare but with an attractive format, the first issue of the magazine opens with an excellent,
full-page sketch of Mark Twain, and the first installment of
his serial *The American Claimant* has a humorous opening
about the weather with an appendix at the beginning for the
reader's choice from select passages of famous literary descriptions of weather for insertion at will. A February plate,
which follows Mark Twain's contribution, has an amusing
set of poems with two sketches about the ideal and the real
of February weather. The following page, which is serious,
is dedicated to the late Philip Bourke Marston, the blind poet
—a close friend of Jerome's and one of the original members
of the "Vagabonds." Marston's poem "Dead Leaves Whisper," with a miniature oval portrait of Marston, fills the page.
Andrew Lang's article, "Enchanted Cigarettes," presents his
dreams—his intentions or memories of romances not written; and the tone is light.

James Payn, editor of the *Cornhill Magazine*, contributes a story, "Her First Smile." W. R. Dunkerley (business
manager, who later wrote novels under the name of John
Oxenham) begins a feature, "Choice Blends," that appears
intermittently, and is a photographic trick of blending nega-
tives to produce a composite picture—in this issue, politicians. Jerome's contribution, "Silhouettes," records rather
grim memories of childhood days on a wild, dismal stretch
of coast, "An 'unken' spot, as they say up North."[3] His memories include a drowning, a near-riot with a victim of the
mob hiding in the Jerome house, and Jerome's father's
coming home to report his own financial ruin in the mines.

Israel Zangwill contributes the funny short story "The
English Shakespeare." "Cynicus" (Martin Anderson) illustrates and hand prints a grim fairy tale. Luke Sharp begins
a series of interviews—as they should be and as they are. This
"Conglomerate Interview with Mark Twain," the featured
writer of the first issue, ends with Oliver W. Holmes' poem
"To 'Mark Twain' (On His Fiftieth Birthday)." The illustra-
tion surrounding it is a funny takeoff with Mark Twain as
"Bubbles" of the famous John Everett Millais painting, sold

to the soap advertiser. Bret Harte's "The Conspiracy of Mrs. Bunker" concludes the articles. Then appears what came to be a well-known tableau; the sketch is of five men lounging before a fireplace; the view, from above, shows the long legs of one reaching to the mantel. The smoke of their pipes forms the heading, "The Idlers' Club." This feature concludes each issue of the magazine, and the staff members speak in their own names with rubrics to give the topics.

In the first issue, Robert Barr, in the guise of idle chatter, presents the editorial policy. The rubric reads: "Robert Barr grieveth that there is no making of new books and magazines in these days." He speaks of bringing youthful talent to the pages, which *The Idler* in fact did; but his suggestion of unknown authors includes Mark Twain, Bret Harte, James Payn, and Andrew Lang. Jerome's paragraph in the column concerns valentines. He talks nostalgically of the fact that valentines are not what they used to be and tells an amusing anecdote or two. Each contributor rambles on his own topic, all speaking in light, satirical tones.

In 1892, W. T. Stead, in the *Review of Reviews'* annual bibliography of periodicals, printed a picture of Jerome and speaks of *The Idler's* "strong team of humourists as its regular staff," and its ambitious illustrations; he adds that *"The Strand* has got a formidable rival in *The Idler* . . . with Mark Twain as its chief attraction, and the Idlers' Club as a special feature."[4]

The "Idlers' Club" throughout Jerome's editorship slightly changes its nature. The first issues begin with only men talking, and their unorganized table-talk covers such subjects as places to idle, holidays, and genius—its environment and its appreciation. The subjects usually lead to anecdotes. Jerome, for example, tells the story of a bishop, one he later reprinted as "The Lease of the Cross Keys" in *John Inger-field and Other Stories.* In a discussion about a British dramatic academy, Jerome takes a positive stand against the others—Zangwill, Burgin, Conan Doyle, Eden Phillpotts, Robert Barr—by maintaining that an academy, while it might not do much for the actors, could at least educate the British playgoer.

In Volume II, the November issue, "Angelina" appears

and speaks at the "Idlers' Club" about the topic of smoking. The next issue adds, besides "Angelina," Mrs. Annie Besant (the Theosophist); "A Lady"; Mrs. Lynn Linton; and Florence Marryat. By Volume III, Israel Zangwill grumbles at the intrusion of ladies, for he thinks they have destroyed the club's freedom: Angelina will not permit them to smoke; tea has replaced whiskey; and "topics" are set instead of being rambling, idle thoughts. The women, however, increase in number to include nine or ten fairly well-known women of the 1890's: Miss Fanny Brough, Miss Quiller-Couch, Miss May Cromelin, Miss Rose Norreys, and others not now generally known.

Moreover, the picture of the young men before the fireplace gives way to a sketch of a library table. Occasionally, the talk centers upon ghosts and the supernatural, apparently an attractive topic of the decade and certainly one to be expected when Mrs. Besant and Sir Arthur Conan Doyle are present. Jerome, intrigued by the supernatural, begins to use it in his fiction. But whatever the topic chosen—"tipping," "love," or "American brashness"—the discussions are lively and amusing; and many a reader must have turned first to the back pages to read "The Idlers' Club."

Another feature in which Jerome had a part besides "The Idlers' Club" was the series "My First Book" in which various authors relate their difficulties in getting into print. Walter Besant, who begins the series in the second number, talks of his book *Ready Money Mortiboy*. Sir Arthur Conan Doyle, Marie Corelli, Rudyard Kipling, Robert Louis Stevenson, Rider Haggard, Sir Arthur Thomas Quiller-Couch (Q), G. R. Sims, and others comprise the rest of the series, which Jerome, in 1897, collected and for which he wrote a preface. Another feature, "Novel Notes," by Jerome, was begun in the May 1892 issue. Jerome also contributed various stories or sketches from time to time—"Silhouettes," the first. "John Ingerfield," "The Woman of the Saeter," "Variety Patter," stories he reprinted later in book collections, are discussed later in this chapter.

Most of the articles in *The Idler* are signed. Some of the features which give zest to the magazine are: a series of rehearsals, written up by G. B. Burgin—one with the D'Oyly Carte Company, a Lyceum rehearsal, Henry Irving's company when Miss Terry was playing Rosamond in Tennyson's *Becket*; "People I Have Never Met," a series by Scott Rankin, presents a photograph of some famous person and a one-page quotation from his work; Sophia Wassilieff runs for several issues her "Memoirs of a Female Nihilist;" George Bernard Shaw, then known as a music critic, writes an article on literary criticism.

Jerome was rightly proud of his contributors, not a few of whom he discovered; for he gave his personal consideration to every manuscript sent in to him. W. W. Jacobs, remembered now for his classic story "The Monkey's Paw" first published stories in *The Idler*. Sir Arthur Conan Doyle, who also wrote for *The Strand*, contributed stories and formed part of "The Idlers' Club." If *The Idler* had first published the Sherlock Holmes stories instead of the Red Lamp stories, the magazine might still be flourishing, in the opinion of Francis Gribble, one of Jerome's young men.[5]

Jerome's contributors not only appeared together in the pages of the magazine but socially as well. In the "pleasant offices in Arundel Street, off the Strand," Jerome and the staff "gave tea-parties every Friday. They were known as the 'Idler At Homes,' and," recalls Jerome in *My Life and Times*, the offices "became a rendezvous for literary London."[6] Francis Gribble, who confirms this statement, says that *The Idler* at homes "were a feature of London literary life at the time. They hardly constituted a *cénacle*—that sort of thing was left to the poets who assembled to read each other their poetry at the Cheshire Cheese. Their note was sociable rather than literary. People who otherwise might not have met were brought together there."[7]

The Idler succeeded so far as circulation was concerned and had a notable staff of contributors. Jerome was joint editor with Robert Barr from the February beginning in 1892 to August 1894, and the sole editor from then to November, 1897. However, in the meantime, Jerome had decided to try a weekly magazine-journal by himself, one which he called *To-day*.

II   To-day

In *To-day*, Jerome combined the features of a magazine like *The Idler*, designed to entertain, with the characteristics of a newspaper—columns of book reviews, theater criticism, political comment, topics of the day, and even financial news, a column that brought disaster to Jerome. "There was no preaching in the columns of *The Idler*. *To-day* was Jerome's pulpit, and one pulpit sufficed for him," according to Francis Gribble in his personal reminiscences.[8]

The paper was a weekly, whereas *The Idler* was a monthly. *To-day* sold for twopence on Saturdays, had an attractive format, and Dudley Hardy, a recognized artist, designed a "Yellow Girl" for the front cover. *To-day*, an illustrated paper, included besides Dudley Hardy, Fred Pegram, Aubrey Beardsley, Lewis Baumer, L. Raven Hill, Phil May, and others as illustrators; but a few photographs also appear in later issues. In the first issue of *To-day*, which appeared November 11, 1893, Jerome begins his series of "Characterscapes"; and the first one was "The Man Who Would Manage." These he later published as *Sketches in Lavender, Blue, and Green* (1897). Phinlay Glenelg—possibly Jerome—contributes "Idle Ideas," which consisted of about fourteen one-line aphorisms, such as, "True humour notes imperfections, only to try to lighten them," or, "While wise wit may educate, high humour must elevate." The feature of the first issue, however, is the first installment of *The Ebb-Tide* a serial by Robert Louis Stevenson and Lloyd Osbourne. "If He Had Lived Today," which features a comic introduction of a classic writer who tries to get his works produced on stage or into print in the modern times, presents a three-page dialogue with Shakespeare about the rejection of *Hamlet* by an actor-manager; and it was probably written by Jerome. For this series, Barry Pain, the humorist, does a skit on Dickens who is reviewed by the *Saturday Review*, and who is labeled by the reviewer as undoubtedly of the "new humourist" school. Although Barry Pain himself had been the first to receive the name-tag of "new humourist," Jerome and the young men who wrote for him soon shared the opprobrium.

Arthur Conan Doyle contributes to the first number a light poem, "A Lay of the Links." "Memoirs of the Late Sir William Hardman," many years editor of the *Morning Post*, appears next. Bret Harte's "The Bell-Ringer of Angel's" begins in this issue. "The Topic of the Week," by Louis Tracy, also in the initial number, considers the British Mission in Afghanistan and speaks for the reform of the prohibitive tariff since it hinders trade. Following these items are unsigned features that were to be ever present in the paper. "To-day," which takes up about two pages, comments on affairs of the day, mostly serious ones. Jerome apparently wrote this column, and the first issue talks of the Coal War, South Africans, the World's Fair in Chicago, and a disturbance of the Salvation Army Band. In sports, the writer tries to promote a bicycle match between England's champion, an amateur, and the French champion, a professional. The English champion is Frank Shorland, Jerome's nephew; and the quarrel between the amateur and the professional reads like the present-day controversies. *To-day*, which carried this sporting cause for some time, finally offered a hundred-guinea challenge cup for a twenty-four-hour race.

The second steady feature, "Stageland," interviews a stage personality; and the first one interviewed is Mrs. Patrick Campbell. The feature tells what is current and good in theaters and in music halls. "Music" provides a weekly review. "The Bookmarker" reviews books, but "The Diary of a Bookseller" later enlarges this function with short notices of more books. "Private Views" tells what is on at the art galleries. "The Bauble Shop," by V. R. Mooney, discusses the week's work in Parliament. "Club Chatter" gives news from the London Clubs, including ideas on men's fashions. "Feminine Affairs," the woman's page, is written by "Penelope." "Oranges and Lemons" contains each week a one-page sketch, or a short story, signed by "The Bell of St. Clements." "Under the Chestnut Tree" presents a page of jokes. The first issue and most other issues run to thirty-two pages—"a wonderful twopennyworth," as Jerome commented, and one can but agree.[9]

In subsequent issues, Jerome adds an answer column to letters to the editor in which he assures a worried correspon-

dent that the circulation of *To-day* has not dropped. He calls
attention to books readers can purchase, such as Israel Zangwill's *Ghetto Tragedies* and his own *John Ingerfield and
Other Stories.* Occasionally, he makes additional comments
about issues that have been taken up by the paper. Aside
from the books he advertises that are publications of serials
run in *To-day* or *The Idler,* there is little advertising in the
paper—only an occasional full-page spread.

Early in 1893, the newspaper announces a serial by
Thomas Hardy that is to appear in the March issue but does
not. However, *To-day* published two special literary supple-
ments, one for November, 1894, and one for the spring of
1895; "The Spectre of the Real," by Thomas Hardy and
Florence Hennicker, appears in the November supplement.
The same issue also features a full-page drawing by Aubrey
Beardsley, "Les Passades." Beardsley, for the regular issue,
contributes the drawing for "Stageland," the page that discusses the theater each week. An article about Beardsley in
the May 12, 1894, issue, "The New Master of Art," gives a
sketch of him and one of his drawings. The spring supplement of 1895 contains Jerome's *Tea Table Talk;* a story by
George Moore, "An Art Student"; and another drawing by
Beardsley.

Other items worth mentioning that appeared regularly are
the short column called "The Old Humour," jokes by Hier-
ocles; a series of amusing articles on new inventions—the
typewriter and the telephone; "De Omnibus," a humorous
column in dialect of the comments of a London bus driver,
by Barry Pain; two articles on chemistry, one of them, entitled "How to Become an Anarchist," explain the different
varieties of dynamite, and the author is Edward Aveling, the
son-in-law of Karl Marx. There is an interview with George
Bernard Shaw. The "To-day" column, which notes the appearance of the new periodical the *Yellow Book,* commends
its Henry James piece and Mr. Davidson's poem; but it
pokes fun at Beardsley's picture of a girl who is playing a
piano in a meadow. "In the City," a regular column on investments, discusses various companies.

Richard Le Gallienne is one of the contributors.[10] Rudyard
Kipling presents "Kaa's Hunting," one of his jungle stories:

and George Gissing's story "Under an Umbrella" opens the January 6, 1894, number. American authors represented in the columns of *To-day* are Bret Harte, Ambrose Bierce, and Bill Nye. (Critics of the "new humor" had accused the "new humorists" of imitating the Americans.)

Jerome's editorial approach to politics is that of a Liberal, and he is critical of the arrogance of British rule in the Empire. His attack on the Turks in their treatment of the Armenians was so outspoken that he was sent for by the Foreign Office. He continued, however, to condemn the Turkish brutalities.[11] He also attacked the Belfast Corporation for cruelty to horses.

The libel suit which forced Jerome to sell his paper grew out of a statement of advice to investors, in the column "In the City," which Jerome did not write. Mr. Samson Fox, a Leeds company promotor, claimed libel. The case "resolved itself into an argument as to whether domestic gas could be made out of water."[12] The case ended with Jerome's losing, the damages being one farthing. The cost was tremendous, and Jerome's bill of nine thousand pounds forced him to sell his interests in both *To-day* and *The Idler*. *To-day* had been from the first a one-man paper, and it quickly died, but *The Idler* continued for some years.

On the whole, Jerome's journalistic career ended with the libel suit of *To-day*. However the essays, stories, and sketches by Jerome which had appeared in various magazines and journals, his own and others, were issued in book form as collections, usually under the name of the first story or sketch. American editions sometimes rearranged the selections so that the title of the book differed though the contents are the same. Jerome chose his illustrators with care, but the sketches are usually the same ones that had appeared in the periodical publication. The drawings, which in several of the collections add to the humor or horror of a tale, were contributions by J. Güich, Hal Hurst, Miss Hammond, A. Frederics, George McManus, Fred Pegram, L. Raven Hill, and Bernard Partridge.

Jerome's collections rarely have a unity of genre. *John Ingerfield* (1893), for example, has three short stories and two reminiscing sketches. *Sketches in Lavender, Blue, and*

Green (1897) divides into two parts, "Tales" and "Characterscapes," which are essays. *Novel Notes* (1893), with a frame device to give it unity, contains anecdotes that are almost short stories. Because of the miscellaneous nature of the collections, the discussions of the volumes in this chapter are by order of appearance in print as books.

III   Novel Notes *(1893)*

In the Prologue to *Novel Notes*, which does not appear in *The Idler*, Jerome begins with a bit of autobiography about his mother's concern at seeing him, as a child, look into the night over the neighboring tombstones and imagine that he saw ghosts. Since his mother was supersensitive, having lost her eldest son when he was six, she imagines that he, too, is ready to join the angels. "The memory of that dingy graveyard . . . came back to me very vividly the other day," he continues, "for it seemed to me as though I were a ghost myself, gliding through the silent streets where once I had passed swiftly, full of life."[13] There follows the pulling out from an old drawer, after the fashion of Sir Walter Scott, a manuscript labeled "Novel Notes": "The book was a compilation, half diary, half memoranda. In it lay the record of many musings, of many talks, and out of it—selecting what seemed suitable, adding, altering, and arranging, I have shaped the chapters that hereafter follow" (4). Jerome explains his right to revise and publish these selections because, of the four joint authors, MacShaughnassy lies dead in the African Veldt; Jephson writes from the Queenslands bush that he has no literary ambitions and thinks there are already too many authors; and

from "Brown" I have borrowed but little. . . . Indeed, in thus taking a few of his bald ideas and shaping them into readable form, am I not doing him a kindness, and thereby returning good for evil? For has he not, slipping from the high ambition of his youth, sunk ever downward step by step, until he has become a critic, and, therefore, my natural enemy. Does he not, in the columns of a certain journal of large pretension but small circulation call me 'Arry (without an "H", the satirical rogue) and is not his contempt for the English-speaking people based chiefly upon the fact that some of them read my books! But in the days of Bloomsbury lodgings and first-night pits we thought each other clever. (preface 4-5)

In the opening chapter of *Novel Notes*, when the narrator remarks to Ethelberta, his wife, that he intends to write a novel, she responds, "Look how silly all the novels are nowadays, I'm sure you could write one" (2). When he adds, however, that he is going to collaborate with three friends, Jerome establishes a framework of a young, not-long married couple and of the husband-narrator who is still convivial with his bachelor cronies in something of the style that marks "The Idlers' Club." Plans for the novel frequently surface through the book, for one speaker or another brings the conversations back to the subject of a heroine—good or bad, for example; the possibility of a novel without a villain; whether the hero should be an author, a stockbroker, an army man. At whatever point the discussion begins, it quickly veers into stories, discussions, or anecdotes about a whole variety of subjects—cats and dogs, ghoststories, dreams, character studies. The framework, only a slight one, offers little movement, except for a decision to hold the next gathering on the couple's houseboat; and this suggestion produces a digression about troubles with a houseboat.

The four characters, however, maintain an identity. Brown's world is upside-down, and he would have heroines ugly; the hero, a scamp. He has an exalted idea of the literary profession. MacShaughnassy tells the fewest anecdotes but is given two good stories, one about a man with a Jekyll-and-Hyde personality who is an aristocrat at one time and low-brow the next. Jephson tells stories, many of which "make you want a little brandy afterwards"; and two of the grimmest stories are his. He has a favorite position while talking: sitting backward on a chair with his elbows resting on the back of the chair. The narrator centralizes all the stories and descriptions and, besides, does his fair share of talking; he also tells many small anecdotes as well as full stories. Structurally, he keeps the discussion and stories regulated like a skillful host; he turns the conversation into levity when spirits drop, or brings levity into balance with a touch of the serious. An obvious example follows the story of Jephson

about his uncle, a chaplain, who attends a criminal about to
be hanged:

> My uncle, failing to make any impression upon him, the governor
> ventured to add a few words of exhortation, upon which the man
> turned fiercely on the whole of them.
> "Go to hell," he cried, "with your sniveling jaw. Who are you to
> preach at me? *You're* glad enough I'm here—all of you. Why I'm
> the only one of you as aint going to make a bit over this job. . . .
> Why it's the likes of me as *keeps* the likes of you," with which he
> walked straight to the gallows and told the hangman to "hurry up."
> "There was some 'grit' in that man," said MacShaughnassy.
> "Yes," added Jephson, "and wholesome wit, also."
> MacShaughnassy puffed a mouthful of smoke over a spider
> which was just about to kill a fly. This caused the spider to fall into
> the river, from where a supper-hunting swallow quickly rescued
> him.
> "You remind me," he said, "of a scene I once witnessed . . ."
> (186).

Some of the topics reflect Jerome's personal preoccupa-
tions, such as a chapter on dogs and on cats; Jerome's probably nostalgic memories of house-furnishing planning with
his bride and the comical household exasperations encoun-
tered by newly-weds; his reflections on the poor; and Jerome's interest in the dual-woman, in a discussion on dreams,
one incident of which he considers as a possible story:

> I dreamt I saw a woman's face among a throng. It is an evil face,
> but there is a strange beauty in it. I see it come and go, moving in
> and out among the shadows. The flickering gleams thrown by
> street lamps flash down upon it, showing the wonder of its evil
> fairness. . . .
> I see it next in a place that is very far away, and it is even more
> beautiful than before, for the evil has gone out of it. Another face is
> looking down into it, a bright pure face. . . . I see the two faces
> again. But I cannot tell where they are or how long a time has
> passed. The man's face has grown a little older, but it is still young
> and fair, and when the woman's eyes rest upon it there comes a
> glory into her face. . . . But at times the woman is alone, and then
> I see the old evil look struggling back . . . (57–58).

This dream becomes the basis for "The Street of the Blank Wall," a first-rate murder story in the collection *Malvina of Brittany.*

A surprising number of the anecdotes are grim stories of evil—horror stories either of revenge, perverseness, or the supernatural. The combination of the humorous and the shocking in *Novel Notes* reminds one of *The Pickwick Papers* in which the interpolated stories form a black contrast to the humor. On the other hand, one must remember that stories of ghosts, doubles, and dual personalities were popular in that period between Robert Louis Stevenson's *Dr. Jekyll and Mr. Hyde* (1886) and Henry James' *The Turn of the Screw* (1898) and his stories of the occult—to say nothing of the Spiritualism of Sir Arthur Conan Doyle and Mrs. Annie Besant, the Theosophist, both members of "The Idlers' Club" in Jerome's magazine. The Drood Murder Case, too, was brought to an actual mock trial by the Dickens' Society during the 1890's, with G. K. Chesterton as presiding judge, G. B. Shaw as foreman of the jury, and some of "Jerome's young men" as honorary jury members. Jerome's ghost stories are convincingly told through the several members who are projecting the novel. MacShaughnassy's story of the perfect dancer, a mechanical creation, has been anthologized in the collections of two twentieth-century crime writers, Dorothy Sayers and Alfred Hitchcock.[14]

In general, the range of interest of *Novel Notes* is broad enough for all tastes; and the collection can still be recommended for good bedside reading. The illustrations by a variety of artists from the staff of *The Idler* brighten the text considerably.

IV   John Ingerfield *(1893)*

Jerome prefaces *John Ingerfield,* a collection of five stories, with a short appeal to the "gentle reader"—also the "gentle critic"—to judge seriously three of the stories: "John Ingerfield," "The Woman of the Saeter," and "Silhouettes." The other two, "Variety Patter" and "The Lease of the Cross Keys," he somewhat bitterly adds, he will "give over to the critics of the new humor to rend as they will." "In Remem-

brance of John Ingerfield, and of Anne, His Wife," the title
story, takes its impetus from the words on an old tombstone
which Jerome locates with what appears to be accurate ge-
ography of London—a tombstone in a little cemetery in
Limehouse. The tale told, purportedly by old people who
knew the Ingerfields, takes the form of a historical short
story.

This is a simple tale about a London tallow merchant, the
descendent of a long line of Northern people traced from
Vikings—a hard-headed race that fights for money, marries
for money, lives and dies for money. John Ingerfield, of the
eighteenth-century generation, marries a woman of fashion
who is to grace his new Bloomsbury home. The marriage is
one of convenience, but each partner respects the other and
also the bargain of their marriage. When the plague strikes
the working people in Ingerfield's business, he, devoted to
his people, tells his wife he must stay with them; but she
must leave London. When he returns to the warehouses, he
is surprised to be joined by his wife who declares in this
way her devotion to him. Together, they alleviate much
suffering, find true love between themselves, and both die,
victims of the plague.

The style of this story seems much like Thomas Carlyle's
style when he is recounting a story—Abbot Samson's, for
example, in *Past and Present*. Since this story is Jerome's
only attempt at a historical one aside from his romantic legends, his affection for the story stems quite possibly from
some childhood recollection of a bit of Limehouse-area
history. The story is slight, but serious.

In "The Woman of the Saeter," a ghost story or a legend
of the Scandinavian lands, two English hunters (the narrator
is one of them) and a Norwegian guide become lost at night
while on a deer-hunt. Stumbling upon a cottage, they are
much relieved until the guide, who recognizes the house as a
haunted one, flees. When the two hunters examine the
cabin, they discover a chest with a bundle of interesting
letters. A ghost story unfolds from the letters written by a
man to his sister in England—letters never mailed since the
wife, jealous of the husband's ghostly visitant, commits a
murder which leads to the husband's killing her. A good

ghost story, it possibly originates from legends heard when Jerome made a trip to Norway with Arthur Conan Doyle and his sister.

"Silhouettes," the third serious sketch, presents child-hood memories by the narrator, presumably Jerome, of life near the sea and in the North. He recalls fishing folk when a body is washed ashore—the hatred of the women for the sea, the suggestion of witchcraft. He remembers the poverty of people and a time when a man fleeing from a mob took ref-uge in the Jerome house. He remembers the fear of the children as they huddle on the stairs while their father braves the crowd storming through the door. Finally, he remem-bers the scene when his father has to tell his mother of his financial ruin and confess, "It's all over, Maggie," . . . "we've got to begin the world afresh."[15]

The remembrances, in sketchy form, are good—as good as Jerome is in the childhood memories of *Paul Kelver*. He is equally successful when his memories of boyhood are fun-ny, as in "Variety Patter," an account of his first wayward attendance at a music hall after having been given money for a Shakespeare performance. As a young reporter, he feels obligated to be a man-about-town; therefore, he frequents the various variety shows. The scenes run in the same vein as in Jerome's earlier *On the Stage—and Off* and in his later *Paul Kelver*.

"The Lease of the Cross Keys" tells a story of a bishop— the confusion and the discrepancies in behavior that arise from the bishop's being mistaken for a drunkard.

This collection, on the whole, is neither more nor less than it pretends to be—an author's own collection of stories that were successfully published in magazines. The whole is a slighter but perhaps an earlier work than *Novel Notes*, whose contents seem to have been written by a more practiced hand. Memories of youth and poverty; idealism in love, the eeriness and mystery in old legends, and the suggestion of the supernatural—they are Jerome at his most popular.

V   Sketches in Lavender, Blue, and Green *(1897)*

Sketches in Lavender, Blue, and Green, which appeared in 1897, contains a group of tales—not quite short stories—

and the feature from *To-day* which Jerome called "Characterscapes." The tales range in subject from love stories to parables, from cat stories to ghost stories; but the best of the stories is "Dick Dunkerman's Cat."

Pyramids, the cat that came to Dick Dunkerman when he was down on his luck, perched like the raven on the corner of his desk just as Dick was contemplating suicide. The cat, who seems to have read his mind, counsels him to wait. Good fortune in the form of a legacy then comes to Dick Dunkerman. As he composes a drama, the cat counsels compromise with his intended theme, suggests that he arrange the plot to please the public, and hints at a change here and there. As a result, Dick's play promises to have a long run. Dick's friends find that Pyramids, when looking at them, makes them abandon their idealism and turn to a cynical realism. One by one, Dick's friends borrow Pyramids for a time: "They give him different names, but I am sure it is the same cat; I know those green eyes. He always brings them luck, but they are never quite the same men again afterward. Sometimes I sit wondering if I hear his scratching at the door."[16]

A few of the stories hark back to Jerome's early Romanticism. "The Materialization of Charles and Mivanway," purportedly told by a landlord on the coast of Cornwall, bears a similarity to accounts of Jerome's own parents in the autobiographical materials. The story is simply that of a very young married couple who quarrel, separate, and then believe either reports or dreams that the other is dead. Upon encountering each other later, each believes for a time that the other is a ghost before reality steps in to provide the happy ending. The prefatory remarks explain: "To confess that the thing really happened—not as I am about to set it down, for the pen of the professional writer cannot but adorn and embroider . . . is, I am well aware, only an aggravation of my offense; for the facts of life are the impossibilities of fiction. A truer artist would have left this story alone . . ." (3). This kind of approach Jerome uses when he is disguising a factually based account.

The other Romantic tale tells a legend of treachery be-

tween Saxons and Danes in East Anglia. The following
paragraph suggests the style:

> And that this tale is true, and not a fable made by the weavers of
> words, he who doubts may know from the fisher-folk, who to-day
> ply their calling among the reefs and sandbanks of that lonely coast.
> For there are those among them who, peering from the bows of
> their small craft, have seen far down beneath their keels a city of
> strange streets and many quays. . . . (179)
> There be some, I know, who say that this is but a legend. . . .
> But such are of the blind, who see only with their eyes. For my-
> self I see the white-robed monks, and hear the chanting of their
> mass for the souls of the sinful men of the town of seven towers.
> For it has been said that when an evil deed is done a prayer is born
> to follow it through time into eternity, and plead for it. . . .
> (181—82)

"The Man Who Went Wrong" and "The Man Who Did
Not Believe in Luck" are semi-humorous tales about a gam-
bler who has a heart of gold but, when converted to Christianity, becomes miserly as well as hypocritical. He is no
longer the Jack Burridge to whom all looked for a handout
and a cheery word in his sinful days. The second story involves the complications of a fellow who is given a Christmas goose, and who runs into bad luck every place he appears with the bird.

A few of the stories are narrated in the loose framework of
after-dinner conversations in which one person begins a
tale, and these are the most plausible of the stories. Jerome
has a knack of recording the exchange of remarks in a convincing way. When the doctor, in "An Item of Fashionable
Intelligence," tells the story of a countess, formerly Mary
Sewell, daughter of a linen draper of Taunton, and "the gossip of the county when I first came here," the others, as he
finishes, keep pestering him with questions of detail which
the doctor does not know and which deflate his intended climax; but, at the same time, they make the telling sound
genuinely true.

The "Characterscapes" are a nineteenth-century version
of the type-study which the seventeenth-century writers

made almost a genre. The titles suggest the subjects: "The Man Who Would Manage," "The Man Who Lived for Others," "The Man of Habit," "The Absent-Minded Man," "A Charming Woman," "The Hobby Rider." Each, however, is made a particular story, a narrative about one eccentric; but the reader feels he can match each case with one of similar excess, oddity, or pertinacity. Most of the descriptions are humorous, as the passage from "The Man of Habit" illustrates:

> Years ago, when I was a young man, I smoked expensive Havanas. I found that I was ruining myself. It was absolutely necessary that I should take to a cheaper weed. I was living in Belgium at the time, and a friend showed me these. I don't know what they are— probably cabbage leaves soaked in guano; they tasted to me like that at first—but they were cheap. . . . I determined to like them, and started with one a day. It was terrible work, I admit, but, as I said to myself, nothing could be worse than had been the Havanas themselves in the beginning. Smoking is an acquired taste, and it must be as easy to learn to like one flavor as another. I persevered and I conquered. Before the year was over I could think of them without loathing, at the end of two I could smoke them without positive discomfort. Now I prefer them to any other brand on the market. Indeed, a good cigar disagrees with me. (282—83)

Jerome's narrative skill in this volume seems to be developing. Characters are more clearly sketched; and, while the style is often the conversational one within the framework, other writers of the period were using this method—to name a few, Joseph Conrad, Henry James, and Arthur Conan Doyle.

VI   The Second Thoughts of an Idle Fellow (1898)

After *The Second Thoughts of an Idle Fellow* appeared in August 1898, the book soon ran into several editions, despite the fact that the fourteen essays that comprise the book had already appeared previously in *The Idler*. The book is a mixed bag of humor, philosophy, reminiscences, and anecdotes. In general, the humor does not predominate as in Jerome's first *Idle Thoughts*; but the ambiguity of "second thoughts" may account for the difference. The essays are longer, less fresh, a bit more heavy-handed than the thoughts of ten years before when the brash and the flip gave zest to the essays. The second thoughts on life, too, are more serious: life is a play, and people as puppets are maneuvered; love is fleeting; success is disillusioning. These are the sombre tones that the book leaves, but the various titles suggest Jerome's usual cheery, sensible comment. Occasionally, the reader finds himself laughing when he has convinced himself that he is about to be bored.

Jerome as an editor has said that the test of a manuscript lies in its first twenty lines. If a writer has had nothing worth saying in those first lines to arrest the attention, the work is not worthwhile continuing.[17] Jerome's opening remarks, like those in Bacon's essays, nearly always attract interest, as the following first lines indicate: "My study window looks down upon Hyde Park, and often, to quote the familiar promise of each new magazine, it amuses and instructs me to watch from my tower the epitome of life that passes to and fro beneath"; "I talked to a woman once on the subject of honeymoons. I said, 'Would you recommend a long honeymoon, or a Saturday to Monday somewhere"; or "Have you ever noticed the going out of a woman? When a man goes out, he says—'I'm going out, shan't be long' "; or "I walked one bright September morning in the Strand. I love London best in the autumn"; or "An old Anglicized Frenchman I used to meet often in my earlier journalistic days, held a theory concerning man's future state, that has since come to afford me more food for reflection." The titles of the essays also intrigue and tease one to read on: "On the Delights and Benefits of Slavery"; "On the Exceptional Merit Attaching to the Things We Meant to do"; "On the Care and Management of Women"; "On the Minding of Other People's Business."

Probably the dominant theme of this group of essays is the discrepancy between one's ideal and reality. For example, in the first essay, lightly introduced by a dialogue of two women trying to make up their minds while shopping, Jerome continues in a semiserious vein to the subject of a young man's idealism:

In my youth, the question chiefly important to me was—what sort of man shall I decide to be? At nineteen one asks oneself this question; at thirty-nine we say, "I wish Fate hadn't made me this sort of man."

In those days I was a reader of much well-meant advice to young men, and I gathered that, whether I should become a Sir Lancelot, a Herr Teufelsdröckh, or an Iago was a matter for my own individual choice. Whether I should go through life gaily or gravely was a question the pros and cons of which I carefully considered. For patterns I turned to books. Byron was then still popular. . . .

The comic and the serious are then mingled:

There are practical difficulties also in the way of him who would play the Byronic young gentleman. He must be supernaturally wicked—or rather must *have been*; only, alas! in the unliterary grammar of life, where the future tense stands first, and the past is formed, not from the indefinite, but from the present indicative, "to have been" is "to be" and to be wicked on a small income is impossible. . . . In the Courts of Love one cannot sue *in forma pauperis*; nor would it be the Byronic method.

"To drown remembrance in the cup" sounds well, but then the "cup," to be fitting, should be of some expensive brand. . . . but when one's purse necessitates that the draught . . . should be of thin beer at five-and-nine the four and a half gallon cask, or something similar in price, sin is robbed of its flavour.[18]

He then adds: "Possibly also—let me think it—the conviction may have been within me that Vice, even at its daintiest, is but an ugly, sordid thing, repulsive in the sunlight; that though . . . it may afford picturesque material to Literature, it is an evil-smelling garment to the wearer . . . (12-13).

In another essay, "Things We Meant to Do," Jerome considers the then-current fad of do-it-yourself activities, grouses a bit at the end product, and weighs it against the virtue of "doing"; "I did not like to suggest to her that before entering upon a difficult task it would be better for young men to *acquire* knowledge and experience: that is so unpopular a theory" (62). From amusing examples of experiences recommended by the magazine "The Amateur," he moves to a sentimental remembrance of his early married days when egg-crates were the furniture:

I have sat on an egg-box at an egg-box to take my dish of tea. I have
made love on egg-boxes. . . . I have gone to bed in egg-boxes
. . . .

How quaint they were, those home-made rooms! They rise out
of the shadows and shape themselves again before my eyes. I see
the knobly sofa; the easy-chairs that might have been designed by
the Grand Inquisitor himself; the dented settle that was a bed by
night; the few blue plates, purchased in the slums off Wardour
Street; the enamelled stool to which one always stuck. . . . Well,
we have got on, some of us, since then, as Mr. Bumpus used to say;
and I notice, when one visits, that some of us have contrived so
that we do sit on Chippendale chairs, at Sheraton dining-tables,
and are warmed from Adam's fireplaces. . . . In the dustbin, I
fear with the cretonne-covered egg-boxes and the penny fans. Fate
is so terribly even-handed. As she gives she ever takes away. . . .
Why did not we know how happy we were, sitting crowned with
sweet conceit upon our egg-box thrones.(65)

The essays contain some sprightly quips: "Every right-
thinking man is an universal lover; how could it be otherwise: You are so diverse, yet each so charming of your kind;
and a man's heart is large. You have no idea, fair Reader,
how large a man's heart is: that is his trouble—sometimes
yours" (92-93); "During her season, London, a harassed host-
ess, has no time for us, her intimates. . . . In the spring, to
be truthful, the great lady condescends to be somewhat vulgar—noisy and ostentatious. Not till the guests are departed
is she herself again, the London that we, her children, love"
(176). Jerome describes a dog taking a man for a walk. And,
when he discusses the complications of the new machine,
the telephone, he strikes a note of sympathy from modern
readers who cope with automated equipment.
    Emerging from the essays is the plea for tolerance for im-
perfect man—tolerance of wives for husbands and vice versa.
The imperfection, or failure, in man leads to the philosophic
question of why man has been created as he is. Jerome wants
to know why, if man is climbing upward in the night, building on his evolutionary pattern of improvement, he did not
start from a higher vantage point. His conclusion is best expressed in the essay "The Delights of Slavery": "Civiliza-
tions, built up with infinite care, swept aside and lost. Be-

liefs for which men lived and died, proved to be mockeries.
Greek Art crushed to the dust by Gothic Bludgeons. Dreams
of fraternity, drowned in blood by a Napoleon. What is left
to us, but the hope that the work itself, not the result, is the
real monument? Maybe, we are as children, asking 'Of what
use are these lessons?' . . . So, perhaps, when we are a
little more grown up, we too may begin to understand the
reason of our living" (148).

VII   Three Men on the Bummel *(1900)*

Three Men on the Bummel or *Three Men on Wheels* in
American editions (1900) recounts more travel adventures of
George, Harris, and "I"—the same trio that had made the
trip up the river in *Three Men in a Boat*. The account is
again based on an actual trip by the three men who ten years
later, with two of the men married and "wanting a change,"
set forth on a bicycling tour of Germany, mainly in the Black
Forest area. A "Bummel," Jerome explains in the last paragraph of the book, "I should describe as a journey, long or
short, without an end; the only thing regulating it being the
necessity of getting back within a given time to the point
from which one started."[19]

The first chapter parallels the opening chapter of *Three
Men in a Boat* in that the three are analyzing what is wrong
with themselves. When all agree on the need of a change,
the problem becomes how to get away without offending
the women or, in fact, without taking the women. After considerable subterfuge on the married men's parts, they are
chagrined to find that their wives are cheerfully anticipating
an absence of three or four weeks from their husbands.

Instead of the chapter on the difficulties of packing, the
new book expands on bicycles—the rage in the 1890's—and
includes a humorous digression about the complications of
repairing bicycles, adding gadgets to them, and Harris' ability to ruin them: "There are two ways you can get exercise
out of a bicycle: you can overhaul it, or you can ride it. On
the whole, I am not sure that a man who takes his pleasure
overhauling does not have the best of the bargain. . . . The
mistake some people make is in thinking they can get both

forms of sport out of the same machine. . . . no machine will stand the double strain" (214).

Before the travelers leave for Germany, Jerome warns the reader: "Anyone who should think that with the aid of this book he would be able to make a tour through Germany and the Black Forest would probably lose himself before he got to the Nore. . . . I do not regard the conveyance of useful information as my *forte*. This belief was not inborn with me; it has been driven home upon me by experience" (235). Then follows an account of Jerome's early journalistic days— possibly exaggerated but probably all too true:

> In my early journalistic days, I served upon a paper, the forerunner of many very popular periodicals of the present day. Our boast was that we combined instruction with amusement. . . . We gave advise to people about to marry—long, earnest advice that would, had they followed it have made our circle of readers the envy of the whole married world. We told our subscribers how to make fortunes by keeping rabbits, giving facts and figures. The thing that must have surprised them was that we ourselves did not give up journalism and start rabbit-farming. . . . We told our readers how many bald-headed men there were in Iceland, and for all we knew our figures may have been correct. . . . We told them how to cure fits in cats. Personally I do not believe, and I did not then believe, that you can cure fits in cats. If I had a cat subject to fits I should advertise it for sale, or even give it away. But our duty was to supply information when asked for. Some fool wrote, clamouring to know; and I spent the best part of a morning seeking knowledge on the subject. I found what I wanted at length at the end of an old cookery book. . . . It had nothing to do with the proper subject of the book whatever; there was no suggestion that you could make anything savoury out of a cat, even when you had cured it of its fits. . . . The paper was not a financial success, it was some years before its time. (235-37 *passim*)

To tie the story back to the trip, he concludes nearly ten pages later, after recounting sundry misadventures of the staff: "Therefore it is that I have come to restrain my passion for the giving of information; therefore it is that nothing in the nature of practical instruction will be found, if I can help it, within these pages" (241).

When Harris is late in catching the train, he reminds Jerome of his Uncle Podger; and the reader is treated to one of Jerome's anecdotes in which the pompous gentleman is mocked by witty boys with Cockney accents:

Many stout City gentlemen lived at Ealing in those days . . . and caught early trains to Town. They all started late; they all carried a black bag and a newspaper in one hand, and an umbrella in the other; and for the last quarter of a mile to the station, wet or fine, they all ran.

Folks with nothing else to do, nursemaids chiefly and errand boys, with now and then a perambulating costermonger added, would gather on the common of a fine morning to watch them pass, and cheer the most deserving. . . . They did not run well, they did not even run fast; but they were earnest, and they did their best. . . .

Occasionally a little harmless betting would take place among the crowd.

"Two to one agin the old gent in the white weskit!"

"Ten to one on old Blowpipes, bar he don't roll over hisself 'fore 'e gets there!"

"Heven money on the Purple Hemperor!"—a nickname bestowed by a youth of etymological tastes upon a certain retired military neighbour of my uncle's—a gentleman of imposing appearance when stationary, but apt to colour highly under exercise.

My uncle and the others would write to the *Ealing Press* complaining bitterly concerning the supineness of the local police; and the editor would add spirited leaders upon the Decay of Courtesy among the Lower Orders, especially throughout the western suburbs. But no good ever resulted.(226)

Sketches such as these mix with anecdotes of George and Harris' having difficulties with the station master, the luggage, the food at a restaurant, and the ordering of things in a foreign language,—the same delightful spoofing that is found in *Three Men in a Boat*.

Comments about the Germans are mostly about their regimentation:

In Germany one breathes in love of order with the air, in Germany the babies beat time with their rattles, and the German bird has come to prefer the box, and to regard with contempt the few uncivilized outcasts who continue to build their nests in trees and hedges. . . .

Your German likes nature, but his idea of nature is a glorified Welsh Harp. He takes great interest in his garden. He plants seven rose trees on the north side and seven on the south, and if they do not grow up all the same size and shape it worries him so that he cannot sleep of nights. Every flower he ties to a stick. . . .

Your German likes the country, but he prefers it as the lady thought she would the noble savage—more dressed. He likes his walk through the wood—to a restaurant. But the pathway must not be too steep, it must have a brick gutter running down one side of it to drain it, and every twenty yards or so it must have its seat on which he can rest and mop his brow.(260-62)

When Jerome observes the German university student, he deplores the practice of dueling. German women come in for remarks, and he comments on the modern German young woman:

If anything can change the German character, it will be the German woman. She herself is changing rapidly—advancing, as we call it . . . . Brilliantly educated she always has been. At eighteen she speaks two or three languages, and has forgotten more than the average Englishwoman has ever read. Hitherto, this education has been utterly useless to her. On marriage she has retired into the kitchen, and made haste to clear her brain of everything else, in order to leave room for bad cooking. But suppose it begin to dawn upon her that a woman need not sacrifice her whole existence to household drudgery any more than a man need make himself nothing else than a business machine. Suppose she develop an ambition to take part in the social and national life. Then the influence of such a partner . . . is bound to be both lasting and far-reaching.

For it must be borne in mind that the German man is exceptionally sentimental, and most easily influenced by his womenfolk. (352)

In the course of discussing foreign language problems, Jerome makes fun of a French textbook, "Ahn's First-Course." He insists the book was written by a witty Frenchman as a satire on the conversational powers of British society. The London publishers thought the satire too subtle but thought it would go well as a textbook. "They altered the title and added a vocabulary, but left the book otherwise as it was. The result is known to every schoolboy" (250). Jerome must have been amused when his own book became a text in German schools. In fact, it is a popular reader where English is studied as a foreign language. *Three Men on the Bummel* has been reprinted and translated and is easily available to readers now. There is fun in *Three Men on the Bummel*. It is probably more entertaining than *The Diary of a Pilgrimage*, but perhaps not as amusing as *Three Men in a Boat*.

VIII   The Observations of Henry *(1901)*

The Observations of Henry, a slight volume of five stories told by the waiter Henry, has the unifying frame of Henry's point of view. Jerome introduces in one paragraph the tales, as "told to me in the long dining-room of the Riffel Alp Hotel, where I once stayed for a melancholy week 'between seasons.' . . . Henry's construction I have discarded for its amateurishness; his method being generally to commence a story at the end, and then, working backwards to the beginning, wind up with the middle. But in all other respects I have endeavoured to retain his method, which was individual; and this, I think, is the story as he would have told it to me himself, had he told it in this order."[20]

In Cockney slang and breezy style, Henry first tells about a ragamuffin girl, reared by Kipper, a newsboy near the corner of Henry's place of work. "Carrots," who has a voice, goes on the music-hall stage after an apprenticeship with Kipper calling newspaper headlines. When she becomes a success on the stage, Kipper, who has been her mainstay, goes away: "You see, me gone, there's nothing to 'amper 'er—nothing to interfere with 'er settling down as a quiet, respectable toff" (23). As Henry rises to jobs in higher-class restaurants, he occasionally meets "Carrots," now a marchioness. "Ever hear from Kipper?" she asks him; and she regrets she can't join Kipper in his hotel proprietorship in South Africa. On the death of the marquis, "Carrots" does a disappearing act. "Henry tells me that at Capetown Captain Kit's First-class Family and Commercial Hotel still runs, and that the landlady is still a beautiful woman with fine eyes and red hair, who might almost be taken for a duchess— until she opens her mouth, when her accent is found to be still slightly reminiscent of the Mile End Road" (36–37).

The second story is about Joe, a youngster who went bad, despite Henry's advising him from time to time. In a holdup of a wealthy home, a maid with a revolver outwits him. Earnest as she is, she seems to like him. She takes him to her master, who, seeing that Joe is not attached to religion or to any principles other than doing a job well, offers to send Joe to the mission field rather than to prison." "It's a dangerous station," says the old gent. "Two of our people have lost their lives there. It wants a man there—a man who will do something besides preach, who will save these poor people we have gathered together there from being scattered and lost, who will be their champion, their protector, their friend" (68–69). Joe and his wife go to Africa: "Later on the Society sent him still further inland, to open up a fresh station; and there it was that, according to the newspapers, the cannibals got hold of him and ate him. As I said, personally I don't believe it. One of these days he'll turn up, sound and whole; he is that sort" (70–71).

These examples are typical of the stories. They are dependent on the surprise ending, the reversal pattern: the wife's becoming self-supporting and the husband the weak, dependent one; a mix-up of dog and baby in the traveling baskets; or the second wooing of the same wife, as in "The Wooing of Tom Sleight's Wife," an idea Jerome puts into the play *Robina in Search of a Husband.*

The personality of Henry comes through with asides suitable to his profession and to his class. Jerome's short stories still sound anecdotal, but this collection bears comparison favorably with the short stories of O. Henry, who was contributing some of his stories to *The Idler* at about this time.

IX Tea Table Talk *(1903)*

Tea Table Talk makes a pleasant afternoon's reading, for its ideas are surprisingly current, and the topics range widely from love to Socialism. Moreover, the book differs from

some of the other collections in that it has unity. It most resembles *Novel Notes,* for a set group of talkers comprise a
colloquium—the same group that had, in fact, presented one
story in *Sketches in Lavender, Blue, and Green.* The group
resembles in style the members that make up the staff in the
novel *Tommy and Co.,* which appeared the following year.
They also resemble "The Idlers' Club" of the feature that
concludes each issue of *The Idler.* The speakers become
familiar to readers of Jerome, and they most likely were derived from his own journalistic staff. The Girton Girl (Cambridge graduate), the Woman of the World, and the Old
Maid speak for women. The Minor Poet, the Philosopher,
and "I," a journalist-humorist-playwright, represent man.

The book, a short hundred and twenty-eight pages, has
chapter divisions without titles, so that often the subject
matter continues from one chapter into the next. The over-
all discussion has to do with woman, her relationship to man,
her position in society; and these topics lead to wider discussions of society, its art, religion, and its future state. The
points of view are determined by the speakers: the Woman
of the World has wealth, position, savoir-faire; the Girton
Girl stands militantly for the equality if not the superiority
of woman. "As a rule, the Girton Girl stands for what has
been termed 'divine discontent' with things in general. In
the course of time she will outlive her surprise at finding
the world so much less satisfactory an abode than she had
been led to suppose—also her present firm conviction that,
given a free hand, she could put the whole thing right in a
quarter of an hour. There are times even now when her tone
suggests less certainty of her being the first person who has
ever thought seriously about the matter."[21] The Old Maid
speaks not as a bitter spinster but as the meek, trembling,
sweet woman who is afraid to have her idealisms shaken;
and, of the six speakers, her opinions seem most dated. The
Minor Poet defends idealism; the Philosopher is somewhat
cynical; and the narrator seldom speaks about the main
topics but serves as an admirable foil, perhaps today's discussion leader. Just enough byplay and banter keeps the
whole discussion from appearing stilted.

A few extracts illustrate the style and subject matter. The group is discussing art:

"Are we so sure that Art does elevate?"

"You are talking for the sake of talking," told him the Girton Girl.

"One can talk for the sake of thinking also,". . . the Minor Poet. "The argument is one that has to be faced. But admitting that Art has been of service to mankind on the whole, that it possesses one-tenth of the soul-forming properties claimed for it in the advertisement—which I take to be a generous estimate—its effect upon the world at large still remains infinitesimal."

"It works down," maintained the Girton Girl. "From the few it spreads to the many."

"The process appears to be somewhat slow," answered the Minor Poet. "The result, for whatever it may be worth, we might have obtained sooner by doing away with the middleman."

"What middleman?" demanded the Girton Girl.

"The artist . . . the man who has turned the whole thing into a business, the shopman who sells emotions over the counter. A Corot, a Turner is, after all, but a poor apology compared with a walk in spring through the Black Forest or the view from Hampstead Heath on a November afternoon . . ." (38–39).

After an anecdote about a man who takes seriously his wife's wish that he continue to treat her as he did during their honeymoon days, the discussion ends as follows:

"You can generally," said the Philosopher, "make people ridiculous by taking them at their word."

"Especially women," murmured the Minor Poet.

"I wonder," said the Philosopher, "is there really so much difference between men and women as we think? What there is, may it not be the result of Civilisation rather than of Nature, of training rather than of instinct?"

"Deny the contest between male and female, and you deprive life of half its poetry," urged the Minor Poet.

"Poetry," returned the Philosopher, "was made for man, not man for poetry. I am inclined to think that the contest you speak of is somewhat in the nature of a 'put-up job' on the part of you poets. In the same way newspapers will always advocate war; it gives them something to write about, and is not altogether unconnected with sales" (21–22).

The Minor Poet later on has another opinion:

"It is a theory of mine that the charming, delightful people one
meets within society are people who have dishonestly kept to
themselves gifts entrusted to them by Nature for the benefit of the
whole community. Your conscientious, hard-working humorist
is in private life a dull dog. The dishonest trustee of laughter, on the
other hand, robbing the world of wit bestowed upon him for public
purposes, becomes a brilliant conversationalist." . . .

"Why, when we meet together, must we chatter like a mob of
sparrows? Why must every assembly to be successful sound like
the parrot-house of a zoological garden?"

"I remember a parrot story," I said, "but I forget who told it
to me" (84–85).

The Philosopher talks about women:

"She is quite content so long as she can detect in herself no tenden-
cy to male vices, forgetful that there are also feminine vices. Woman is the spoilt child of the age. No one tells her of her faults. . . .
Incompetence to pack her own bag or find her own way across a
square and round a corner is deemed an attraction. Abnormal ignorance and dense stupidity entitle her to pose as the poetical ideal
. . . . The marvel to me is that, in spite of the folly upon which
they are fed, so many of them grow to be sensible women."

"Myself," remarked the Minor Poet, "I find much comfort in the
conviction that talk, as talk, is responsible for much less good and
much less harm in the world than we who talk are apt to imagine"
(107–08).

This commentary might have made an admirable conclusion,
but the following closes the book:

"I had no idea," said the Woman of the World, "you were a Socialist."

"Nor had I," agreed the Minor Poet, "before I began talking."

"And next Wednesday," laughed the Woman of the World, "you
will be arguing in favour of individualism."

"Very likely," agreed the Minor Poet. "The Deep moans round
with many voices."

"I'll take another cup of tea," said the Philosopher (128).

The topics of *Tea Table Talk* might have been the subject of editorials or of serious articles, for they will always be controversial ones. In this conversational, colloquial discussion, Jerome catches, however, a larger reading public than he would have had he written in the formal manner of a serious thinker.

X Idle Ideas in 1905

Idle Ideas in 1905 is the third and the last volume to bear Jerome's cognomen of the "Idler." The twenty-one unrelated essays cover topics usually phrased as questions, such as "Are We as Interesting as We Think We Are?" "Are Early Marriages a Mistake?" "Do Writers Write Too Much?" "Should Soldiers Be Polite?" "Is the American Husband Made Entirely of Stained Glass?" "The White Man's Burden! Need it be so Heavy?" "How Many Charms Hath Music, Would you Say?" In these essays, Jerome seems more outspoken than in previous essays—he is less hesitant to speak of government policy, of specific social wrongs, and even of particular tendencies in art. The tone remains light, inoffensive, good-humored; but, occasionally, Jerome is didactic.

Fashion, society, behavior come in for light ridicule, with particular jibes at the crowded "at homes," where the small talk can be difficult. "Should Women Be Beautiful?" presents a man's opinion of the beauty columns in women's magazines: "In future years there will be no need for a young man to look about him for a wife; he will take the nearest girl, tell her his ideal, and, if she really care for him, she will go to the shop and have herself fixed up to his pattern. . . . Match-making mothers will probably revive the old confession book. Eligible bachelors will be invited to fill in a page: 'Your favourite height in women,' 'Your favourite measurement round the waist,' 'Do you like brunettes or blondes?' The choice will be left to the girls."[22]

European carnival time is commented upon in "When Is the Best Time to Be Merry?", and some amusing customs are described. France, Belgium, and their customs are topics of two or three more of the essays, the titles of which do not suggest travel notes. Of the Belgian markets, Jerome writes:

> They are one babel of bargaining, these markets. The purchaser selects a cauliflower. Fortunately, cauliflowers have no feelings, or probably it would burst into tears at the expression with which it is regarded. It is impossible that any lady should desire such a cauliflower. Still, out of mere curiosity, she would know the price— that is, if the owner of the cauliflower is not too much ashamed of it to make a price.
>
> The owner of the cauliflower suggests six sous. The thing is too ridiculous for argument. The purchaser breaks into a laugh.
>
> The owner of the cauliflower is stung. She points out the beauties of that cauliflower. Apparently it is the cauliflower out of all her stock she loves the best. . . . (57)

In the essay "Do Writers Write Too Much," Jerome finds how convenient and how time-saving is the synopsis of a serial novel that he has in part missed. With more foresight than he knew, he concludes: "My fear is lest this sort of thing shall lead to a demand on the part of the public for condensed novels. What busy man is going to spend a week of evenings reading a book when a nice kind sub-editor is prepared in five minutes to tell him what it is all about!" (102).

"Creatures that One Day Shall Be Men" contains an interesting insight into English opinion of Russia in 1905: Jerome writes of the Russians:

> They strike the stranger as a child-like people, but you are possessed with a haunting sense of ugly traits beneath. The workers— slaves it would be almost more correct to call them—allow themselves to be exploited with the uncomplaining patience of intelligent animals. Yet every educated Russian you talk to on the subject knows that revolution is coming.
>
> But he talks to you about it with the door shut, for no man in Russia can be sure that his own servants are not police spies. . . .
>
> "It is gathering," [my friend] said; "there are times when I almost smell blood in the air. I am an old man and may escape it, but my children will have to suffer—suffer as children must for the sins of their fathers. We have made brute beasts of the people, and as

brute beasts they will come upon us, cruel, and undiscriminating: right and wrong indifferently going down before them. But it has to be. It is needed."

It is a mistake to speak of the Russian classes opposing to all progress a dead wall of selfishness. The history of Russia will be the history of the French Revolution over again, but with this difference: that the educated classes, the thinkers, who are pushing forward the dumb masses are doing so with their eyes open.(145–47)

In the essay about the White Man's Burden, Jerome discusses the Yellow Peril of the era: "The present trouble in the East would never have occurred but for the white man's enthusiasm for bearing other people's burdens. What we call the yellow danger is the fear that the yellow man may before long request us, so far as he is concerned, to put his particular burden down. It may occur to him that, seeing it is his property, he would just as soon carry it himself" (235).

Writing about Americans, Jerome attacks wives who spend their time in Europe and expect their husbands to remain at home, to work, and to be faithful. "Is the American husband made entirely of stained glass?" he asks; and he naively pretends to think the women travelers are all widows, traveling to forget.

An essay on Wagnerian opera has the usual fun with the stilted conventions, but is a bit more pointed in attacking Wagner's particular theory that acting and singing could both be well done in opera—in short, that opera could substitute for all the arts. This concept Jerome ridicules, and he concludes that "the object to be aimed at by the wise composer should be to make us, while listening to his music, forgetful of all remaining artistic considerations" (224).

American Wives and Others (1904), with illustrations by George McManus, contains the same essays included in *Idle Ideas in 1905* but with different titles. Twenty-two of its twenty-five essays are the same as *Idle Ideas in 1905*, and the other three appear in *The Angel and the Author.* Cut versions of some of the essays appear in Dover Publications' *The Humorous World of Jerome K. Jerome* (1962).

XI   The Passing of the Third Floor Back *(1907)*

The first three stories of the collection entitled *The Passing of the Third Floor Back* deal with supernatural intervention, yet all are curiously different in the nature of the supernatural. "The Passing of the Third Floor Back," which is far more famous in Jerome's play version, deals with a mysterious stranger who, a sort of Christ, enters the lives of ordinary boardinghouse occupants who are despicable in their petty ways and reforms them by finding the best in them. His presence, whether he is appearing to the policeman or to Stasia, the "slavey," reminds each of his past when he was a better person. The constable notes the stranger's peculiar looks. "Funny," added the constable, gazing after the retreating figure of the stranger. "Seen plenty of the other sex as looked young behind and old in front. This cove looks young in front and old behind."[23] Miss Devine, encountering him notes: "His voice had a strange ring of authority, compelling her to turn and look upon his face. Yes, it was true, the fancy that from the first had haunted her. She had met him, talked to him—in silent country roads, in crowded city streets, where was it? And always in talking with him her spirit had been lifted up: she had been—what he had always thought her"(38–39).

The second short story, "The Philosopher's Joke," like the story following it, involves the drinking of a vial of miraculous liquid. The setting is the room in Königsberg where Immanuel Kant had often sat discoursing of "the universe as a result of our own perceptions." Three married couples, each acquainted with the narrator, all admit that in that room they sat discussing the fact that, married twenty years, each had become unhappy with his marriage, and had thought someone else of the group more suitable than his or her own partner. A strange little gentleman offers them all a glass of a chemical he has prepared which will allow them to reappear as they were twenty years before but with the simultaneous knowledge of the present. After taking the liquid, each ponders curiously the pros and cons of his or her marriage choice and in the end is more satisfied after this review. When the couples awake the next morning, they discover that, strangely, they have all had the same dream; but the evidence of their broken wine glasses remains as a mysterious contradiction to their belief that they were dreaming.

The third story of the supernatural, "The Soul of Nicholas Snyders," presents a curious type of visitant, one difficult to identify as either good or evil. The old miser, Nicholas, may, by drinking a magic draught, enjoy according to the proposition made to him by the stranger, the happiness of youth if he can get someone to exchange souls with him. Jan, eager for money and Christina, the pretty ward of Nicholas, agrees to the exchange. Of course, Jan now becomes mean and miserly while Nicholas grows unrecognizably kind. Christina no longer pleases Jan, and old Nick himself falls in love with his charge. Finding that Christina loves Jan in spite of his strange, unpleasant behavior, Nick sacrifices himself by drinking the stranger's second draught and taking back his meanness so that Christina may have a loving Jan. In Jerome's dramatic version, this story has often been used as a Christmas play; in the drama, Jerome adds a child to turn away a beggar who, at the end of the play, would have maliciously prevented the second taking of the miraculous draught.

"Mrs. Korner Sins Her Mercies" has a title derived from a colloquial expression meaning that one is ungrateful for the good one possesses. The story is about the type of situation suggested by the title, for a wife thinks her husband not so exciting and manly as the stage drunk who is witty. The husband becomes drunk and so very unpleasant that he frightens his wife as well as himself. He finally persuades his wife, however, that he was bringing her to her senses by showing her the reality as opposed to the false picture presented by the stage drunk.

"The Cost of Kindness," a sardonic little story, tells of a parochial quarrel of a minister with his dissatisfied congregation. The formality of politely apologizing for misunderstandings produces in the clergyman the belief that his former opponents have had a change of heart and really want him to stay. The cost of kindness proves dear, as he stays. The story is amusingly told but is little more than an anecdote. "The Love of Ulrich Nebendahl" tells a legend of a war hero of the French and German wars, who finds love of country in self-sacrifice when all think him a traitor.

The best of the stories is probably "The Philosopher's Joke." As individual stories, the ones in this collection tend to be longer, have more suspense, a more decided climax, and better character delineation than the conversational anecdotes that Jerome calls "sketches," "observations," or "after-dinner talk" in some of his other collections.

The six stories in this collection range from the colloquial talk of "The Passing of the Third Floor Back" to the more sophisticated conversation in "The Philosopher's Joke" to the almost archaic style of the legend "The Love of Ulrich Nebendahl." In both "The Philosopher's joke" and "The Love of Ulrich Nebendahl" Jerome emphasizes his theory of the multiple attractions in love and the different qualities in different people, as well as the differences that time makes in the qualities one loves.

XII   The Angel and the Author *(1908)*

The Angel and the Author can best be described as a collection of commonsense sayings about commonplace subjects. Most of the essays are reprints of those in *American Wives* (or *Idle Ideas in 1905*) or from selections that had previously appeared in newspapers and magazines. The style is anecdotal, gently satirical. For example, on "Man and his Masters," Jerome writes: "There is one thing that the Anglo-Saxon does better than the 'French, or Turk, or Rooshian,' to which add the German or the Belgian. When the Anglo-Saxon appoints an official, he appoints a servant: when the others put a man in uniform, they add to their long list of masters."[24] The anecdote that follows of the Swiss post-office officials who refuse to release the baggage of Jerome and two friends who are on a walking tour through the Tyrol brings the kind of laughs that the adventurers in *Three Men in a Boat* produce.

On the subject of the independent woman, Jerome appears in these essays more sympathetic to the working woman or to the single girl than he does in his plays appearing in the same decade. Some of the statements he makes about such women are used verbatim in the plays. "It has been said that the difference between men and women is this: That the man goes about the world making it ready for the children, that the woman stops at home making the children ready for the world" (224). This statement becomes the speech of Wolff Kingsearl in *Miss Hobbs*. However, in the essay Jerome adds, "Will not she do it much better for knowing something of the world, for knowing something of the temptations, the difficulties, her own children will have to face, for having learnt by her own experience to sympathize with the struggles, the sordid heart-breaking cares that man has daily to contend with?" (224) He continues with this comment on the same subject:

Civilization is ever undergoing transformation, but human nature remains. The bachelor girl, in her bed-sitting room, in her studio, in her flat, will still see in the shadows the vision of the home, will still hear in the silence the sound of children's voices, will still dream of the lover's kiss that is to open up new life to her. She is not quite so unsexed as you may think, my dear womanly madame. . . .

There is no reason to fear that the working woman will ever cease to think of husbands. Maybe, as I have said, she will demand a better article than the mere husband-hunter has been able to stand out for. . . . Maybe the bridegroom of the future will not say, "I have married a wife, and therefore I cannot come," but "I have married a wife; we will both come." (226)

The conclusion is that which Jerome also uses in *The Master of Mrs. Chilvers* and in *Anthony John*.

In light moments, Jerome talks of styles in dress, of umbrellas, and of the heroine of the problem play in an essay in the style of *Stage-Land*. But the new woman of the post-Ibsen era is different from the type of heroine described in the melodramas of Jerome's first satire. For example, he says of the new heroine:

She is a careless woman. She is always mislaying that early husband. And she has an unfortunate knack of finding him at the wrong moment. Perhaps that is the Problem: What is a lady to do with a husband for whom she has no further use? If she gives him away he is sure to come back, like the clever dog that is sent in a hamper to the other end of the kingdom. . . . Her surprise at meeting him again is a little unreasonable. She seems to be under the impression that because she has forgotten him, he is for all practical purposes dead. (87–88)

Since Jerome makes considerable use of the supernatural in various stories, it is of interest to read what he has to say of ghosts and Spiritualism in this volume:

My real stumbling-block is the spirit himself—the sort of conversation that, when he does talk, he indulges in. I cannot help feeling that his conversation is not worth the paraphernalia. I can talk better than that myself.

The late Professor Huxley, who took some trouble over this matter, attended some half-dozen *séances*, and then determined to attend no more.

"I have," he said, "for my sins to submit occasionally to the society of live bores. I refuse to go out of my way to spend an evening in the dark with dead bores". . . .

I would give much to believe in ghosts. The interest of life would be multiplied by its own square power could we communicate with the myriad dead watching us from their mountain summits. . . .

May not we be but blind children, suggests the poet [Zangwill], living in a world of darkness—laughing, weeping, loving, dying—knowing nothing of the wonder round us?

The ghosts about us, with their god-like faces, it might be good to look at them.

But these poor, pale-faced spooks, these dull-witted, table-thumping spirits: it would be sad to think that of such was the kingdom of the Dead. (174 and 179)

Witty, genial, sometimes touching the profound, these essays retained Jerome's popularity with the public.

XIII   Malvina of Brittany *(1916)*

The title of the collection *Malvina of Brittany* is from the opening story, a tale of the supernatural, which is a combination of legend and whimsical make-believe. In a plot that suggests television plots of fifty years later, Jerome's young aviator of World War I picks up a beautiful young girl alone at midnight on the seacoast in Brittany. She insists she is Malvina of the ancient fairy kingdom of King Heremon of Ireland and Queen Harbundia of Brittany. The young aviator's uncle and Professor Littlecherry, a medievalist, confirm the accuracy of her information; and they help the young couple surmount various complications resulting from Malvina's innocent use of her supernatural powers. The story is pleasant fantasy, told with tongue-in-cheek seriousness.

"The Street of the Blank Wall," which could have come from the pen of Sir Arthur Conan Doyle, is a story of suspense, with murder, blackmail, and mistaken identity, that was developed from a dream which Jerome hinted had possibilities in *Novel Notes*. Jerome maintains suspense—London on a foggy night with a mysterious signal from a lighted window, a mysterious stranger, a woman's frightened face. The bachelor company has been talking: "I think it was in connection with a discussion on Maeterlinck. It was that sudden lifting of the blind that had caught hold of me. As if, blundering into an empty theatre, I had caught a glimpse of some drama being played in secret."[25]

"His Evening Out," a fairly long story, collects the evidence from park policemen, waiter, housekeeper, and various witnesses to Mr. Parable's running away with his cook. The accounts of the witnesses, told in their varied, characteristic speeches, show Jerome at his best. The story, a natural for dramatization, became a successful play—in England as *Cook* and in America as *The Celebrity*.

"The Lesson" deals also with the mysterious, the occult. The story hints at Theosophist ideas, and the first person narrator, like Jerome in his youth, has been a clerk for commissioners for India. The narrator meets a strong, successful Dutch Jew who employs him during his first European vacation. The wealthy Jew seems attracted to him; and in a lonely Swiss cabin, where the Jew has gone to die, he talks to the narrator of a past existence: "This world was a school, so he viewed it, for the making of men; and the one thing essential to a man was strength. One gathered the impression of a deeply religious man. In these days he would, no doubt, have been claimed as a theosophist; but his beliefs he had made for, and adapted to, himself—to his vehement, conquering temperament. God needed men to serve Him—to help Him. So, through many changes, through many ages,

God gave men life: that by contest and by struggle they
might ever increase in strength" (219).

When the narrator has grown older, he becomes attracted
to a crippled boy who is somewhat skillful as a painter. The
narrator feels that the boy may be the reincarnated Dutch
entrepreneur. Taking the young artist to the same Swiss
cabin, he learns that the young man, too, believes in a previous existence. Some of the characteristics of the powerful Jew remind the reader of Dr. Hal, of *Paul Kelver*. The
idea of the incomplete God is later developed by Jerome
in his last two novels. Jerome has probably also been influenced by the beliefs of Mrs. Annie Besant, the Theosophist who sometimes appeared in "The Idlers' Club," and
by Sir Arthur Conan Doyle and his Spiritualism.

"Sylvia of the Letters" bears an initial resemblance to the
novel *Tommy and Co.*, for in each work a bachelor takes in
an impish little girl. In the short story, she is the orphaned
daughter of a woman he has always idealized, but Jerome
compounds the situation by having the bachelor also take in
the orphaned son of a second woman he has loved. He
wishes the boy and girl to marry, but they can scarcely tolerate each other. When the bachelor dies, the young people
go their separate ways; but each corresponds pseudony-
mously with an ideal admirer. In searching for the ideal
correspondents, the two find that, in reality, the correspon-
dent is the formerly unsatisfactory foster sibling. Chosen
over the dream, reality, even with its acknowledged imperfections, satisfies.

"The Fawn Gloves," which is more a sketch than a story,
is about a poor clerk who falls in love with a poor working
girl whom he meets in the park. She wears gloves continually. When he proposes, she removes her gloves to show a
badly scarred hand, disfigured by some kind of factory work;
and he is repulsed, but ashamed of his reaction. He leaves
London for a short time; but, after inquiring of a doctor, he
learns that her affliction can be cured. The young man,
though, searches in vain through London for the girl of the
fawn gloves. The story reads like an early sketch of Jerome's:
it lacks character development and plot, and its sentiment
comes close to bathos.

Of the whole collection, "The Street of the Blank Wall" merits preserving—and perhaps "Malvina of Brittany" as a playful fantasy. As for the sketches, essays, stories in these collections, they were written for entertainment for a wide reading public; and they are the work of a journalist. The meanings are clear on the surface. While they may make one think about the mystery of death, the kinds of love, and the possibilities of ghosts, the writings do not conceal hidden meanings nor depths to be discovered on a second or third reading. Jerome had a recognized skill in recording dialogue, and from some of the complications in story or sketch he reworked the material into plays. When Jerome wished to develop a serious thesis, he turned to the novel. For his humor, he is best in these essays and travel accounts; in these, he both entertains and amuses.

CHAPTER 4

The Idler as Dramatist

I Jerome's Dramatic Career

IF the modern reader does not know Jerome K. Jerome as the author of *Idle Thoughts of an Idle Fellow* or as the humorist of the best-seller *Three Men in a Boat*, he may have heard of *The Passing of the Third Floor Back* (1908); for his play had sensational runs in both England and America and became one of the most popular plays in the first quarter of the twentieth century, and is still revived from time to time.[1] The theater had opened the literary world to Jerome K. Jerome; indeed, activity and interest in drama run through his professional career. From clerking in the Euston railroad station, Jerome's first show of independence was to join a traveling troupe. Playing every part from low-comedy roles to the First Walking Gent. at thirty-five shillings a week, he covered the touring circuit of Great Britain, including the East End and Surrey-side theaters of London. In *On the Stage—and Off* (1885), written after time had distanced by a few years his immediate disillusionment, Jerome records his observations of stage life and theater roles in a book which entertained his contemporaries and provides now an authentic stage history. His second book about the theater, *Stage-Land* (1890), also provides a valuable account of that period before Ibsen, Shaw, and Wilde when nothing good seemed forthcoming from the English theater world. *Playwriting*, an anonymous work of 1888, published by The Stage Office and a handbook for would-be dramatic authors, probably comes from Jerome's pen.[2] The book gives practical advice in a pleasant, informal style by "a dramatist."

Jerome had closed the door on acting as a profession after three youthful years on the stage; but he turned, naturally enough, to the writing of plays while he was making his way into the field of journalism. About *Barbara* (1886), his first play to be accepted for production, Jerome recalls in *My Life and Times* that, in his youth, managers seldom read plays by unknown authors. Rose Norreys, an actress Jerome knew, took his play to Charles Hawtrey, manager of the Globe Theater, who "liked my little play immensely. There was only one fault he had to find. It was too short. I record the fact as being the only known instance in the history of the stage of a manager suggesting to an author that his play was not long enough" (134). Jerome, upon Hawtrey's advice, refused the offered one hundred pounds and kept the rights. The play, a one-act comic drama, starred Cissy Grahame as Barbara. The Augustin Daly company in America also ran the play successfully, and amateurs found it a favorite for years.

Adaptations filled some of the need for plays for the theaters, and Jerome wrote *Sunset*, adapted from Tennyson's poem, "The Two Sisters"; *Fennel*, an adaptation from François Copée's *Le Luthier de Crémone;* and *Honour*, from Sudermann's *Die Ehre* (called *Birth and Breeding* in the Edinburgh production). *Fennel* introduced the handsome Allan Aynesworth to the London stage, though on the opening night Jerome agonizingly listened while Aynesworth forgot his big speech and extemporized. "Bits of it, here and there, were mine; most of it his own; a good deal of it verses and quotations that, I take it, he had learnt at his mother's knee."[3]

Allardyce Nicoll in his *History of Late Nineteenth-Century Drama* commends Jerome's *Sunset* (1888) as an advance over the old melodramas with some poignancy in the characters and increased skill in presenting episodes in which the conflict arises not from outside events but from the "clash of nature with nature, or of thought with thought."[4] When Jerome, however, produced *Woodbarrow Farm* (1888), his first full-length play—four acts, then the fashionable length—A. B. Walkley, the reviewer, accused him of using a stereotyped stage farmer and taunted Jerome with passages from his satire in *Stage-Land*.[5]

Jerome featured Gertrude Kingston as the adventuress in the play. Together they gave it at a trial matinee, a useful system that allowed one to rent a theater for about a hundred pounds to try the play on the public. When this performance was successful, the play was bought by John Hare. Dan Frohman took it to America. When Jerome took the play on tour in England, a Mary Ansell played the ingenue. J. M. Barrie, producing a play in London at the time, needed a leading lady; and Jerome, who suggested Miss Ansell, released her from his cast. She became the wife of J. M. Barrie.

Jerome wrote in the following years before the close of the century a few more plays, some of them mere curtain-raisers presented before main plays; some written in collaboration with Addison Bright, Eden Phillpotts, Adrian Ross, and Haddon Chamber. One play, *Biarritz*, was a musical comedy. George Bernard Shaw, reviewing the performance at the Prince of Wales Theatre, said of the chorus of girls, "Two minutes of *Biarritz* would reconcile a Trappist to his monastery for life."[6]

The period was one in which authors received little publicity. Jerome tells of an occasion when a lady once asked him why he didn't write a play: "I told her I had written nine: that six of them had been produced, that three of them had been successful both in England and America, that one of them was still running at the Comedy Theatre and approaching its two hundredth night."[7] But Jerome's plays often had stellar casts—actors and actresses, not now remembered, who were leading lights in the theater of the 1890's; and Jerome knew the actors and actresses both professionally and as friends. Their names fill the books of memoirs of the period, and photographs of them can be found in histories of the theater. Gertrude Kingston, E. H. Sothern, Frederick Harrison, and Eric Lewis played in *Woodbarrow Farm*; Lena Ashwell, Arthur Playfair, Cyril Maude, and Fanny Brough in *The Prude's Progress;* Cissy Graham, W. E. Penley, Gertrude Kingston, and Bernard Partridge (contributor to *Punch* and Jerome's illustrator for *Stage-Land*) in *New Lamps for Old;* in America, Ada Rehan, John Drew, and Mrs. Griffiths played the leads in some of his plays. In fact, authors wrote for specific actors or actresses. Jerome speaks of reading his play to Mrs. Patrick Campbell, and he wrote three plays for Marie Tempest, and he adds:

two . . .she never played in, and the third she wishes she hadn't. It was her own fault. She wanted a serious play, and I gave her a serious play. She loved it when I read it to her. "Esther Castways" was the name of it. She was magnificent in it, and on the first night received an ovation. But, of course, the swells wouldn't have it. She had made a groove for herself; and her public were determined she should keep it. We ought to have known that, all of us. I didn't get on with her at rehearsals. I wore a red suit. I rather fancied it myself; but somehow it maddened her; and I was obstinate and wouldn't change it, though she offered to buy it off me that she might burn it.[8]

When the Nazimovas, having fled from Russia, came to Jerome, he took them to Herbert Beerbohm Tree; and they together arranged a benefit performance for them at the Haymarket Theatre and later arranged their passage to America.

The theater of the 1880's and 1890's was moving out of the earlier period of melodrama into a more Realistic drama to replace the artificial language and the loosely constructed plots of early Victorian drama. The French theater of Eugene Scribe had innovated the *piéce-bien-faite*. Alan S. Downer explains in his handbook *The British Drama*: "The well-made play is just what its name implies, a tidy, logical, machine-made structure replacing the older jerry-built structure of romantic drama. . . . Every situation must be prepared for well in advance, must grow logically out of what has gone before. . . . The careful handling of exposition must now be done 'realistically.' . . . Audiences quickly developed an insatiable taste for the 'new realism' and hearing their problems discussed upon the state."[9] The problems were usually of marriage and love, of course. Jerome, with his ear tuned to the speech of the people, supplied convincing dialogue. In *The MacHaggis*, written with Eden Phillpotts, their heroine shocked the critics with her realism; she rode a bicycle and smoked a cigarette. "The Devil must have been in us," Jerome recalls. "Up till then, only the adventuress ever smoked a cigarette. In the last act, she said 'damn.' She said it twice. Poor Clement Scott nearly fell out of the *Daily Telegraph*. . . . No one dreamed the day would come when Mrs. Pat Campbell would say 'bloody.' But it is an age of progress, we are told."[10]

George Bernard Shaw who wrote many reviews of the plays of the 1890's, criticized sometimes gently and sometimes harshly the plays of Jerome. Shaw could not tolerate *The Rise of Dick Halward* (at the Garrick in 1895) for the "pessimism of Mr Jerome K. Jerome and his school . . . who says 'We are all hopeless scoundrels; so let us be kind and gentle to one another!'" (I, 236). Shaw's statement about the cast confirms what has been said about the plays and actors:

Fortunately for Mr Jerome, the five parties to this unexampled stage effect were artists no less popular than Miss Marion Terry, Miss Annie Hughes, Mr Willard, Mr Esmond, and Mr Barnes. If Mr Jerome will try it at the Independent Theatre with five comparatively unknown performers, he will probably be made acutely conscious of his own originality. . . . I find it very hard to believe that Mr Jerome, in writing this play, or Mr Willard in producing it, had any other object than to make money in the cheapest possible way. . . . [Our managers] deliberately select melodramas of the Surrey and Marylebone types, and engage first-rate performers to present them at west end houses at west end prices . . . . Take this play of Mr Jeromes . . . [it] is arrant fustian, better than the fustian of twenty years ago, no doubt, but still, judged by the literary and artistic standards of today, very sorry fustian. (I, 238, 239, 240)

On the other hand, Shaw found it an "unspeakable relief to get away from Sardou to Mr Jerome K. Jerome whose *Prude's Progress* is much better than its name. . . ." He found it a "shrewd, goodnatured, clever cockney play . . . interesting and amusing all through, with pleasantly credible and pleasantly incredible incidents, ending happily but not fatuously; so that there is no sense of facts shirked on the one hand nor of problems stage-solved on the other" (I, 147). Of *The MacHaggis*, Jerome and Eden Phillpott's farce of 1897, Shaw stated, "It is an intentionally and impenitently outrageous play . . . but its absurdity is kept within the limits of human endurance by the Jeromian shrewdness and humanity of its small change" (III, 66).

In the late Victorian period, Ibsen received his first recognition in England with Henry Arthur Jones' wild adapta-

tion of *A Doll's House* in 1884. Jerome, recalling his own
adaptation of Sudermann's *Die Ehre*, remembers Jones'
adaptation in which "Helmar took the forgery upon himself,
and the curtain went down on Nora flinging herself into his
arms with the cry of 'Husband'; and the band played 'Charlie
is my Darling.' . . . 'A charming author,' was the first
verdict passed upon Ibsen by London."[11]

But Henrik Ibsen, played close to the original (continu-
ously championed by G. B. Shaw in reviews) by J. T. Grein's
Independent Theatre productions, shocked England in the
1890's with his portrayal of social evils. Jerome, telling of
the actress Alma Murray, indicates the changing British reaction when he writes that she might have been a leading
actress but for her roles in Ibsen's plays: "In those days the
feeling against Ibsen was almost savage, and no player
prominently connected with his plays was ever forgiven."[12]
Jerome's *New Lamps for Old*, of 1890, contains its parody of
Ibsen's *Doll House* with a loud bang of the street door just
before the curtain falls; and in 1904, in one of his humorous
essays, Jerome satirizes the heroine of the problem play in
"The Problem of the Problem Plays."[13] *Miss Hobbs* (1899),
or "The Kissing of Kate," Jerome's first big money-maker,
produced first in America by Charles Frohman, makes a
comedy from the subject of the independence of the new
woman. Jerome, as he moves into the new century, becomes
concerned with the problems of society.

While Jerome was writing some of these popular comedies, he was, at the same time, editing the magazine *The
Idler* and his weekly *To-day*, besides being involved in two
lawsuits. Nevertheless, he also initiated the project of a
dramatists' theater; but the plans did not work out although
Jerome had thought them feasible. After Jerome's court case
which forced him to sell his interests in his papers, he returned to writing essays, travel books, stories, novels, and
more plays. The first of the plays of this period, *Miss Hobbs*
(1899), opened in New York with Annie Russel and Mrs.
Gilbert as "Auntie." The play ran for nearly two hundred
performances. It played in London; then the Princess
Paulowa successfully took the play to the Continent—to
Russia, Germany, and Italy.

John Ingerfield, a play adapted from Jerome's own short story, had a good run in New York in 1899: *Susan in Search of a Husband* (1906), was Jerome's story adapted in America by Eugene Presbrey; for Jerome's own adaption is called *Robina in Search of a Husband*, and it appeared at the Vaudeville Theatre, London, in 1913. Jerome's play comes from his story "The Wooing of Tom Sleight's Wife" in *The Observations of Henry*. *The Passing of the Third Floor Back* (1908), also dramatized from Jerome's own short story, marked the peak of Jerome's dramatic fame. He read the play to David Belasco in New York, but Belasco became nervous about its religious theme; and, since Johnston Forbes-Robertson wanted to stage it, Jerome and the Forbes-Robertsons produced it in England first. Sir Johnston Forbes-Robertson played the Stranger, and his wife, Gertrude Elliott, played Stasia, the "slavey", though Jerome's daughter Rowena appeared in the part in the Provinces. *The Passing of the Third Floor Back* made its trial performance at Harrowgate where the audience, familiar with Jerome's *Three Men in a Boat*, mistook it for a farce. Blackpool, with a less sophisticated audience, reacted differently; and Forbes-Robertson wired to Jerome in London that "Blackpool understands it and loves it." The play then ran at the St. James' Theatre, where it was a box-office success.

Everyone talked about the play: ministers quoted from it, clubs discussed it, and sophisticated critics deplored it. *Punch*'s Owen Seaman was condescending in his review with a few guarded compliments—"Not that Mr. Jerome's work has been tactlessly done"—but he thought the play lacked variety and that the author did not attain sufficient fun in his first act.[14] Max Beerbohm's criticism for the *Saturday Review* treats the play scathingly with such phrases as "tenth-rate writer . . . prolific of his tenth-rate stuff" and "vilely stupid." Of course, what grated was "that the play is so evidently a great success. . . . Greater enthusiasm have I seldom seen in a theatre. And thus I am brought sharply up against that doubt which so often confronts me: what can be hoped of an art which must necessarily depend on the favor of the public—of such a public, at least, as ours? . . . Twaddle and vulgarity will have always the upper hand."

The unkindest cut of all comes in Beerbohm's final statement, "Well, I suppose blasphemy pays."[15] On the other hand, Clayton Hamilton, of *The Forum* considered the play "a parable that is sweetly intentioned and sincerely written."[16] Both he and other reviewers commended the device used in one scene:

Students of the difficult art of stage-direction will be interested by a device that is employed in the presentation of this piece. It is necessary, for reasons of reality, that in each of the dialogues the Passerby and his interlocutor should be seated at their ease. It is also necessary for reasons of effectiveness in presentation, that the faces of both parties to the conversation should be kept clearly visible to the audience. . . . The producer therefore adopts the expedient of imagining a fire-place in the fourth wall of the room— the wall that is supposed to stretch across the stage at the line of the footlights. A red-glow from the central lamps of the string of forelights was cast up over a brass railing such as usually bounds a hearth; and behind this, far forward in the direct centre of the stage, two chairs were drawn up for the use of the actors.(441)

Forbes-Robertson's sister-in-law *insisted* that the play go to New York, where it ran 216 performances in 1909 and 1910 before going on tour to major cities as far west as Kansas City. Theaters begged for hold-over performances, which advance bookings did not allow. Perhaps the proper tribute with which to close a discussion of this play is the double-edge compliment which Jerome quotes. Matheson Lang had taken the play to the Orient, and "In China, a most respectable Mandarin came round to see him afterwards and thanked him. 'Had I been intending to do this night an evil deed,' he said, 'I could not have done it. I should have had to put it off until to-morrow.'"[17]

In October, 1908, the same year of *The Passing of the Third Floor Back*, Jerome satisfied his audiences who wanted humor with *Fanny and the Servant Problem*, a pleasant comedy about an aristocrat who marries a show-girl on the continent. When she proves to be related to his entire staff of servants, complications arise. Miss Fannie Ward played the part of "Lady Bantock," the title Jerome gave the play for its American performances. The play proved popular,

too, in translations in Europe; but it was not well received
in London.

Class problems and hypocrisy in religion are humorously
touched upon in *Fanny and the Servant Problem*. *The Master of Mrs. Chilvers* (1911), which Jerome labels "An Improbable Comedy," deals seriously with the question of
women's rights and presents the new woman quite attractively and quite fairly. The nearest of Jerome's plays to a
problem play, it makes a creditable plea for woman's independence; however, the solution involves Mrs. Chilver's
capitulation to her husband's point of view.

Esther Castways, written for Marie Tempest in 1913,
proved not very successful, though Jerome had the satisfaction of seeing his daughter Rowena perform in it. The
play deals with Americans and mill reform bills, but neither
the Americans nor the British liked it. World War I interrupted Jerome's play *The Great Gamble*, which unfortunately had a German setting. *Cook* (or *The Celebrity*) (1913),
from which Jerome did not expect much, received favorable
reviews; but it had to wait for a good run from abroad in
1917. It dramatizes the short story "His Evening Out" contained in the collection *Malvina of Brittany*. Now, this play
would probably be judged the best of his comedies. The
novel *Tommy and Co.* Jerome adapted to the stage, along
with a few other short stories he had written. Some of them,
also, like *Lady Bantock*, were turned into musical comedies;
but the last major play Jerome wrote was an adaptation of
his story "The Soul of Nicholas Snyders" into a play which
sometimes bore that title and was sometimes called *Man or
Devil*. Lionel Barrymore's production in New York in May,
1925, was a failure, but the play has subsequently been
presented successfully as a Christmas play.

In the June, 1925, *Harper's Magazine* Jerome contributed
an article, "Chronicles of a Playwright." The article contains
pictures of Jerome as well as a photograph of Forbes-Robertson in *The Passing of the Third Floor Back*. This article
became a chapter in *My Life and Times*, which Harper published in 1926. In a sense, Jerome's career began and ended
with his interest in the theater.

Today, with the exception of *The Passing of the Third*

Floor Back, Jerome's plays are little known and virtually un-obtainable. *The Passing of the Third Floor Back* appears in Samuel French's current catalogue of plays, but none of the others do; and the Dramatist's Play Service of 1967-68 lists none of them. About twelve were published as reading editions, but even they are scarce. Jerome's plays served their purpose in providing good theater for the audiences of their time, but they were not intended to be considered as literature.

The plays that are discussed in greater detail have been chosen to show not so much fine drama but Jerome's thinking, the themes he developed, and the skill with which he presented his ideas. Chosen from his early, middle, and late works, they represent both the comedy and the serious drama he wrote.

II   Miss Hobbs

Miss Hobbs, which appeared in 1899, develops the theme of the new woman and shows, in a seriocomic vein, the influence of Ibsen's *A Doll's House*. A comedy in four acts, the play presents a newly married couple, Beula and Percival Kingsearl; an engaged couple, Millicent Farey and George Jessop; Miss Hobbs, militantly single, who is charming with *"the manner of an exceptionally important and busy Princess"*;[18] Miss Abbey, an old-maid aunt who is sympathetic to marriage; Wolff Kingsearl, a dashing bachelor who arrests his travels to visit the husband who also has the name of Kingsearl; Charles, the fifteen-year-old servant; and Captain Sands, skipper of the yacht. The well-made plot of the play makes use of only one coincidence, one not too improbable: Percival Kingsearl, the young husband, and Wolff Kingsearl, the traveler, have the same surnames. The similarity of their names accounted for their having noticed each other during their school days; therefore, their friendship has a logical origin.

The play centers on Miss Hobbs, who, friend of the two young women, has indoctrinated them with views of the independent woman. The girls, who think highly of her, have become dissatisfied with their young men; and, as the play opens, Aunt Abbey has been called in to listen to Beula defend her independence and Percival to state his rights. The aunt comes too late, however, for Beula has already decided to leave Percival, Millicent has broken her engagement to George Jessop, and both girls have packed to move to Miss Hobbs' residence. At this awkward moment, Wolff Kingsearl arrives. When Percival explains the absence of his wife, he complains of the horrid Miss Hobbs, whom he has not met; and he challenges—even bets—Wolff that Wolff will kiss Miss Hobbs before the month has ended. Wolff appears indifferent; but while Percival and George are out of the room, a young woman arrives to get Beula's overnight bag. Wolff, through the boy Charles, has learned that the pretty young woman is Miss Hobbs. Miss Hobbs, seeing his name on a note, assumes him to be Beula's Mr. Kingsearl. When Wolff Kingsearl flirts with her, Miss Hobbs has her opinion of men confirmed. Thinking to expose him to Beula as unfaithful, she encourages Wolff to come to her house, where she privately sets a trap for Beula to see her supposed husband making love to her.

The scheme fails when Beula announces that the man is not her husband, much to the extreme embarrassment of Miss Hobbs; and she is furious when the notebook Wolff has dropped reveals the bet as to the "kissing of Kate." At this point the direction of the action changes: the couples reunite, and the intent of the plot of the play is to bring Miss Hobbs and Wolff Kingsearl together. On a yacht, Wolff Kingsearl deceives Miss Hobbs into thinking the boat is adrift in a fog. He insists on her doing woman's work of cooking and serving while he does the man's work. Both argue the question of woman's place in society, but his supposed demonstration that woman's place is in the home is not accepted by Miss Hobbs, and the two separate, angry with each other. The final scene opens with the couples and Miss Abbey plotting again to bring Wolff and Miss Hobbs together. Only the announcement by Wolff that he must leave for foreign parts makes Miss Hobbs realize her love for him. Left alone, the two agree that she will willingly tend to woman's homemaking while he will live the more dangerous, exciting life to support her.

Miss Hobbs provides both comic intrigue and a thesis. The intrigue has a triple strand—the confusion not of twins but of duplicate names; the problem of how men may get back their estranged women; and the taming-of-the-shrew idea, which Jerome intended to acknowledge or reinforce with the subtitle "The Kissing of Kate." In this play, Miss Henrietta Hobbs must be convinced that a woman cannot do a man's job and that "Man bustles about the sea and land getting the world ready for the children. Woman bustles about the home getting the children ready for the world. What's the difference," in the words of Wolff (52).

Miss Hobbs, however, presents her case. At the turn of the century, the independent woman was not just a shrewish Kate, willful with a choleric temperament. Like Ibsen's Nora, Miss Hobbs finds that woman's lot lacks satisfaction, indeed, her position resembles that of a general servant. Even Wolff, in talking to Percival, blames society: "'The thing your women over here suffer from is having nothing to do all day but sit about and think, and that's just the way to think wrong. They know nothing of the world. Work, the whole explanation of life, is a sealed book to them. What they want is to be taken out of this doll's house you call civilization and made to face facts" (43). As for Miss Hobbs, she protests: "I don't object to work. . . . It's the kind of work I object to. The man keeps all the interesting work for himself, and sets the woman to wash up the dishes" (52). Miss Hobbs has observed somewhat bitterly, too, the double-standard of behavior between men and women; and her experience has given her a biased view—"brought up by an aunt who had buried two husbands, both of 'em wrong uns, and who took it out by going about, giving lectures on the social problem. . . . Seems to have been a regular heavy-weight. Jolly hard lines on the girl, I call it" (42), Jessop explains.

George Bernard Shaw, arguing a decade later the same questions in his comedy *Getting Married* (1908), also provides witty arguments between an engaged couple, the parents, a celibate Anglican priest, an unmarried aunt, and her admirer for twenty years. Jerome's play was presented earlier when the suffragist movement was not quite so strong. In 1911, in *The Master of Mrs. Chilvers*, Jerome, too, devotes a whole play to the question of woman's independence; but in *Miss Hobbs* his intent is as much to amuse as to instruct; and he is less consistent in his treatment of the thesis than is Shaw.

At the beginning of *Miss Hobbs*, Charles, the fifteen-year-old servant, has worn another suit on top his livery because "I hate the sight of it. Why should I be labelled a slave all over," he says to Miss Abbey, who dismisses his complaint with a laugh; but, when his mistress, Beula, hears his complaint, she answers: "We are all slaves, Charles, of one kind or another. You wear your livery, I mine," as she turns her wedding ring round her finger (5). Aside from this hint at the beginning and some complaint from Beula—justified, surely—that Percival has burned her bicycle bloomers, the serious argument is delegated to the dialogue of Miss Hobbs and Wolff Kingsearl. Jerome overlooks the fact that Aunt Abbey, who is single, might have contributed something to the discussion. Instead, she belongs to the stock world of comedy and to the private memories of Jerome of his own aunt with her bobbing curls at the side of her head. She is the pothering, kind, affectionate lady who serves as the confidante.

In Shaw's play, every speech displays a facet of the central argument; and the contributions of the maiden aunt bear as much weight as the protests of the young fiancée. On the other hand, a standard literary history refers to Shaw's *Getting Married* as scarcely a play at all but as a dialogue, some of it tedious.[19] Jerome's play is not tedious because of the action. Jerome's acting career had taught him not to forget the audience satisfaction in humorous stage business; therefore, *Miss Hobbs* provides bits of fun, such as the displays of vanity before the mirror when Wolff, thinking himself alone, is followed by Miss Hobbs, who thinks *she* is alone in primping before a mirror. The funny business of climbing in and out of windows; of forgetting a hat; of trying on a hat too small; of sliding in and out of the room just in time to avoid someone else—all are old but amusing tricks. Two amusing conversations stand out—Captain

Sands' comments about taking the yacht into possibly bad weather, remind one of Captain Goyles' remarks in *Three Men on Wheels*—the kind of "Idler" thoughts Jerome was famous for; and the threat that Wolff may actually have to tune the piano, his pretense for calling at Miss Hobbs' house, provides amusing dialogue.

Jerome recounts how, in his early days of acting, one gesture brought down the house. He was acting the bit part of a policeman, but his sole speech was to pronounce a fallen victim dead. At one performance, instead of examining the body, he simply leaned forward, sniffed once, and said "dead." The gag was thereafter left in the book. This is the kind of effectiveness of which Jerome is aware, and the script leaves much opportunity for an actor's ingenuity. For example, the audience and Miss Hobbs have almost been converted to Wolff's point of view in Act II; and after Miss Hobbs has tenderly bound up his bleeding hand, the audience expects her capitulation. She turns on the second step of the ladder, after shaking hands in an amicable goodby and adds: "Oh, Mr. Kingsearl, you dropped this climbing over the fence (*hands him his betting book open at the page*). I hope you'll all three enjoy your dinner at Delmonico's on July 6th" (*She runs up and disappears, leaving him standing at the foot of the ladder with the open book in his hand*). *Wolff*: "Damn! (*Curtain*)" (54).

Miss Hobbs illustrates the well-made play with characters balanced and with action and motivation prepared for or explained, such as Miss Hobb's biased view of men. The interest of the play does not depend entirely on what novel situation will arise next, but on the revelation of the flaw in Miss Hobb's character that explains why she acts as she does; for Jerome has reached a stage in his writing when he can make characters stand out, Miss Hobbs in this case, for her own individuality. The author makes clear, however, that the relationship of the young women to Miss Hobbs is not Lesbian. Percival says to Wolff: "What's to be done with a woman who makes it her business to go about ruining other people's lives, who estranges lovers and breaks up homes?" *Wolff*: "In my part of the world, we store that sort

in sacks. Public opinion—*Percival: interrupting*, "No, no!
I don't mean that sort of bad. The woman who does mischief
from a sense of duty" (16).

The play does not seem so dated as some of Jerome's, perhaps because of its theme of the liberated woman. It probably could still be played by amateurs with very little
updating of the lines. In the history of the drama, *Miss Hobbs*
contributes in the movement of bringing drama into a closer
relation to the reality of the social world.

III   Fanny and the Servant Problem

Fanny and the Servant Problem (1908), which appeared
shortly after Jerome's successful *The Passing of the Third
Floor Back*, is a romantic comedy—"A Quite Possible Play
in Four Acts," the subtitle reads. The play deals with the
improbable situation of a young lord who marries a Paris
chorus girl who, when she arrives at Bantock Hall in Rut-
landshire, finds that she has "married into a family that
keeps twenty-three servants, every blessed one of them a
near relation of my own," as she explains to Newte, her
ex-manager.[20]

The play opens with two elderly aunts who are awaiting
the return of their nephew and his bride. He has not informed his bride of his title. The servants also await the new
mistress; in fact, they are preparing for her, for the Bennet
family who staff the house—as unpleasant a Nonconformist
family as ever graced the stage—feel the humiliation of
having an actress degrade the standing of Bantock Hall.
Indeed Mr. Bennet is nailing a few mottos to the walls of her
room for her edification. When Vernon Wetherell, Lord
Bantock, enters with his bride, she pleases with her charm,
her youth, her graciousness. When Bennet, the butler, enters,
he addresses Vernon and Fanny as "my lord" and "my lady."
To the pained surprise of both the butler and the bride,
Fanny and her uncle recognize each other. The Bennet
family leaves her alone, thinking her shocked at the discovery of the station into which she has married.

The Bennets, loyal to the Bantock household, which they
have dominated for years, have decided that Fanny is not
to be found unworthy of the place: they will improve her.

In their hypocritical way, they set about sobering her dress and her morals. Fanny sends for her old manager, Newte, who, in trying to be helpful when Vernon had made enquiries about her past, had supplied an imaginary uncle as a bishop in New Zealand and another as a judge in Ohio. Complications arise and are avoided as members of the family and servants pass in and out, but the situation comes to a climax when fourteen girls from the chorus Fanny had belonged to arrive to give her a surprise. When Bennett decides to serve them in the kitchen and Fanny hears of his intention, she demands that they be brought upstairs; and she gives them a pleasant hour. After they leave, she gives Bennet a check for the whole family and, in the presence of all the household, fires the entire staff of servants— all Bennets. Then she confesses before her husband, Newte, and the aunts that the Bennets were her family from whom she had fled. The household, considerably disturbed, retires for the night.

The last act opens with Newte trying to light the fire. The aunts come down hungry, for no breakfast has been sent to their rooms. When Vernon appears to share Newte's boiled eggs, Bennet, as imperturbable as ever, suddenly appears as if he had not been dismissed. Fanny enters, ready to leave if Vernon expects it; but he defends her. Bennet, who approves her spirit, thinks her now capable of heading the household affairs. Vernon asks Bennet's permission to marry his niece, a gesture that all agree is the sole recognition of family relationship to be made. The aunts then confess that the first Lady Bantock, whose imposing picture has been an inspiration to Fanny, was, after all, only a butcher's daughter.

The clash of interests in the play keeps suspense at a high level. Upon Fanny, the varied situations converge. She must juxtapose her past as an actress to her new role as Lady Bantock; she must cope with the lies about her nonexistent relatives; she must deal with her existent relatives who offer exposure as the alternative to conformity; she must show loyalty to the chorus from which she came; and most important of all, she must establish whether or not Vernon's love can transcend the knowledge of her origins. Fanny also does a bit of self-analysis that fits in with Jerome's constant re-

minder of the dual personality of each of us. "I'm two
persons," she says to Dr. Freemantle, the understanding
family physician. "I'm an angel . . . We'll say saint—or
else I'm the other thing. . . .It has always hampered me;
never being able to hit the happy medium" (33).

Jerome manages to get the maximum effect out of each of
the confrontations that arises: Lady Bantock, dressed puri-
tanically by the Bennet maid as the symbol of her conformity; Newte, the chorus manager with his cigar, confronting
Bennet; the fourteen chorus girls, members of "Our Empire," sharing champagne and cookies with the elderly
aunts; and the high point of all, Fanny's dismissal of the
whole Bennet family as she confesses her relationship to
them.

Besides the comic effect, Jerome strives for a strike against
class distinctions. In an indirect manner, Fanny tries to find
out from Vernon what he would think if he knew she belonged to his family of servants. He has just laughed and
said, "Well, one hardly marries into one's own kitchen."
Fanny takes this up. "Isn't that rather snobbish? You say
they're more like friends than servants. They've lived with
your people, side by side, for three generations, doing their
duty—honourably. There's never been a slur upon their
name. They're 'high-principled.' You know it. They've better manners than nine-tenths of your smart society, and
they're healthy. What's wrong with them—even from a lord's
point of view?" (55). Vernon's innocent answer is that he
has married Fanny, not one of his servants.

Vernon Wetherell, Lord Bantock, who is one of Jerome's
weaker characters, is not only spineless but smug. When
Fanny has been talking with Dr. Freemantle and Vernon
enters, he remarks to Dr. Freemantle, "Doesn't she talk
well?" Even *soto voce*, which stage directions do not indicate, the remark would be intolerable. Vernon also gives
considerable evidence of being the snob his wife accuses
him of being; but he makes the right statements for the
happy ending of the play when he insists that the "county"
have "got to be told in any case. If you are here, for them
to *see*, they'll be able to understand—those that have got
any sense" (38). Readers of Jerome's short story "The Ob-

servations of Henry" will recall that "Carrots" of music-hall fame, befriended by a character quite like Newte, grew tired of the upper class into which she had married, saying: "It's just like a funeral with the corpse left out. . . . Serves me jolly well right for being a fool."[21] We could almost predict such a future for Fanny were the play an "open-end" drama rather than the well-made play. A good actor, perhaps, might salvage Vernon's part by his acting.

The indistinguishable old aunts—indistinguishable even to Vernon, which is a bit preposterous since they have reared him from childhood—function with Dr. Freemantle as a means for the opening exposition. They provide commentary on the main characters and on family history, and they wander in and out of the room in a frightened way that could be amusing. The butler, Bennet, is the stock type of the stage butler; but the rest of his family is almost farcical. On the whole, the success of the play depends upon a capable actress to play Fanny. She appears poised from the first, but she develops by the end of the play into a woman of character who is capable of renouncing for the sake of integrity. *Fanny and the Servant Problem*, not so good a play as *The Celebrity* (or *Cook*) has, nevertheless, enough comedy of situation to provide, with bringing up-to-date a few lines, a lively modern comedy.

IV   The Celebrity (*or* Cook)

The Celebrity (1917) derives from Jerome's clever story, "His Evening Out," in the collection *Malvina of Brittany*. In the short story, witnesses at court tell the incidents; and the main characters—the celebrated John Parable and his cook,—are only talked about. Their words are quoted as evidence by the park policeman, the girl at the kiosk, a waiter, the housekeeper, the boy at the newspaper office, and by Mr. Parable's manservant. The plot in story and play remains exactly the same; but the characters who carry the dialogue in the play are the principles in the action: John Parable, famous writer and speaker for the Fabian Society, Socialism, various other causes; Miss Bullstrode, woman champion of the same causes and engaged to John Parable; Miss Dorton, the weepy, devoted secretary; Archibald

Quincey, newspaper reporter and Parable's friend; Illingworth, Parable's manservant; Mrs. Meadows, housekeeper
of his country cottage; Comfort Pryce, Parable's pretty young
cook and the heroine of the play; Joseph Onions, her former
friend; and Sunnybrook Jim, who goes bail for Parable. In a
reading of the play, something seems to have been lost from
the short story. The particular slant of each of the witnesses,
all of whom are from the working class, gave a zest to the
story that the middle-and upper-class characters in the play
version lack. However, good actors and actresses—Jerome
had them,—could probably give more sparkle to the lines
than a reading of the play offers.

A comedy romance, the play has no overtones of women's
rights, no serious discussion of the kinds of love, and even
the matter of social rank, in the marriage of one of the upper
classes to his servant, has just one spirited defense when
Comfort Pryce, the pretty little cook, defends herself to
Mrs. Meadows: "I've heard him from a dozen platforms
ridiculing class distinctions, saying it's all nonsense. Besides, my people have been farmers for generations. What
was Miss Bullstrode's father but a grocer? He kept a hundred shops instead of one. That only makes it a hundred
times worse. Why shouldn't I?"[22]

The play is a situation comedy based on a celebrity's not
recognizing his own cook Comfort Pryce when he meets
her all dressed up, in the park. They decide on an evening
together, dinner and dancing, which ends in Parable's fighting with Comfort Pryce's former boyfriend. When John
Parable is arrested, he—thinking only partially of the embarrassment to the Socialist movement for which he speaks—
gives the name of his newspaper friend, Archibald Quincey,
at the police station instead of his own. Comfort Pryce, in the
meantime, has asked Sunnybrook Jim to go bail to get
Parable released from jail.

At home, his bevy of admirers and supporters await him—
Quincey, the militant Miss Bullstrode, Miss Dorton, and
Illingworth. The discussions and accusations that follow
his arrival home leave Parable frantic. Miss Bullstrode persuades them that Parable needs a rest in the country. Parable,
who in the meantime has just made the private discovery

that his attractive friend of the evening is his cook, surprises his friends by his agreeableness to the suggestion: he closes Act I with a seeming afterthought: "Tell Cook to get ready immediately. I'm taking her with me" (32).

Act II concerns the development of love between Comfort Pryce and John Parable and the appearance, one by one, of his followers at the country cottage. Each one has his own solution about how to keep Parable from having to appear in court or about how to keep him from marrying his cook. Accusations are made to the cook, who privately sacrifices herself by sending for her former boyfriend, Joseph Onions, and by agreeing to marriage with him if he admits to the court that he began the fight.

Act III provides the counterscheme of Joseph Onions, who, by blackmail, extracts the promise of a thousand pounds—five hundred to take the desired court position and five hundred from Miss Bullstrode to promise to marry Comfort Pryce, whose reputation, he maintains, has been damaged. All problems seems to be settled. Parable, glum, plans a trip to Scotland and then marriage with Miss Bullstrode, the perfect political companion. Comfort Pryce resigns herself to her sacrifice. Through Quincey, Comfort learns of the blackmail, and indignantly frees herself from her promise to her former friend. John Parable, in turn, insists on nobly serving his jail sentence; and the curtain falls as Comfort and Parable happily decide to take the trip and to be married in Scotland.

The characters have distinct personalities, but they are almost standard by now in Jerome's repertoire of people. Miss Bullstrode, who resembles Elizabeth Spender of *The Master of Mrs. Chilvers* or the unreformed Henrietta Hobbs of *Miss Hobbs*, is the unfeminine woman of little grace or sensitivity. Quincey, the blustering, good-hearted, practical man is like Newte of *Fanny and the Servant Problem*. Comfort Pryce, a favorite type of Jerome's, is the forward, pretty girl of the lower ranks whose beauty, common sense, and love for a man raise her to a higher position. She lacks the cockney accent; but, otherwise, she resembles Stasia, "Tommy," Ginger, "Carrots," and Fanny of various plays and stories. She is, however, the only one of the characters to develop during the play: from a pert servant, partly amused by her catch, she makes a genuine move of magnanimity toward John Parable when she sends the note to John Onions promising to marry him because of what he can do for Parable.

Jerome's opening exposition is masterly. Illingworth, the long-time servant, answers the questions of Miss Dorton, the secretary, both of whom cannot account for the morning and overnight absence of Parable, who keeps a regular schedule. Others arrive—Miss Bullstrode and Mr. Quincey for an interview—and conversations reveal that Parable did not speak at his appointed meeting the night before. The audience is thereby prepared for his entry and explanation: *"John Parable's head looks in. Seeing that there is nobody in the room but Quincey, John Parable enters and closes the door. John Parable is a distinguished looking man of about forty. He wears an overcoat with the collar turned up, and a very new-looking billy-cock hat"* (15). The questions that follow, begun partly about the hat, which is not the type known in his photographs, introduce the necessary exposition of the mystery of what had happened the night before. A smooth, well-planned opening, it arouses curiosity, satisfies it, and leads to the next mystery of who the young lady is—one presently solved when Illingworth informs Parable that Cook has only just arrived from an unexplained absence. Jerome's skill in this logical exposition demonstrates an advancement over *Fanny and the Servant Problem* or *Miss Hobbs* in which extraneous aunts are provided as listening ears or as explainers who clarify the opening situations.

The complications of the love plot, in which "the course of true love never does run smooth," strengthen the attractiveness of the play since both Comfort Pryce and John Parable make sacrifices due to consideration for each other. The obstacles to the romance, which the friends think they have removed by their scheme, make a fine contrast to the unselfishness of the two main characters, so that the ending is an effective, pleasant recognition scene.

In this play Jerome's stage directions are helpful to the reader. For example, upon Miss Bullstrode's first entry, the stage directions read: *"Illingworth goes out. After a*

*moment, Miss Bullstrode's vigorous voice is heard outside
. . . and the door is burst in, rather than opened, and
Miss Bullstrode enters. She is a woman of, say, five and
thirty. In the costume of a lady, she would be attractive;
but dressed (with exception of the trousers) as a gentleman
with eccentric taste in clothes, she is not at her best. Under
a bowler hat, she wears her hair strained back from her
forehead, and uses a stout walkingstick"* (7). Or of Illingworth: *"One does not know his Christian name, butlers
never having Christian names except in the bosom of their
own families. Illingworth, a bachelor, who has been with
the Parable family all his life (but for which he would not
be there now, being deeply opposed to the present John
Parable's political opinions), has probably, if he ever had
one, forgotten it. He is the typical butler, imperturbable,
chronically resigned, and constitutionally sad. He had come
to give an eye to the fire"* (6).

The play has a great deal of movement although it has
only two settings, for people are constantly coming in and
out. The second act, set in the country cottage where Parable
is trying to be alone with the Cook, provides good comedy
with the cumulative gathering of the characters. *The Celebrity* is Jerome's last comedy, and its success surprised him.
Bombings over London during the run closed the theater, but not before Jerome had received praise from the
critics. Reviewers were pleased to see the humor of Jerome
again without the jeremiads or touches of sentimentality of
his more serious plays.

V The Master of Mrs. Chilvers

*The Master of Mrs. Chilvers, An improbable Comedy
imagined by Jerome K. Jerome,* is not so improbable, which,
of course, Jerome understood. The "improbable" in the title
allows in this well-made play for the circumstance, or coincidence, that the woman most likely to be the candidate in an
election just happens to be the wife of Geoffrey Chilvers,
a member of Parliament and president of the Men's League
for the Extension of the Franchise to Women. Given this
improbability, the plan then revolves around the question
of what will happen if his wife, Annys Chilvers, runs for

office against him, which she decides to do. The audience, understanding the possibilities, settles down to enjoy the clashes—the suspense of the contest, what will happen if she wins, what will happen if she loses. In the process, a good debate occurs; partisanships form, dissolve, and reform; but the ending leaves all contented.

Jerome chooses for his setting, besides the Russel Square opening, the East India Dock Road constituency and the town hall in East Poplar, where he lived as a boy. The cast, a large one, consists of eleven women and eight men; and each is delineated with a paragraph description (after the fashion of George Bernard Shaw's copious comments in his stage directions) in which Jerome effectively epitomizes different approaches to the question of women's rights. A few selections illustrate Jerome's method: "Geoffrey Chilvers, M.P. . . . in sympathy with the Woman's Movement: 'not thinking it is coming in his time'"; "Phoebe Mogton, thinking more of politics than of boys. But that will probably pass"; "Annys Chilvers, a loving wife, and (would-be) affectionate mother. Many thousands of years have gone to her making. A generation ago, she would have been the ideal woman: the ideal helpmeet. But new ideas are stirring in her blood, a new ideal of womanhood is forcing itself upon her"; "Mrs. Mountcalm Villiers—She was getting tired of flirting. The Woman's Movement has arrived just at the right moment"; "Elizabeth Spender—She sees woman everywhere the slave of man: now pampered, now beaten, but ever the slave"; "Ginger—Whose proper name is Rose Merton, and who has to reconcile herself to the fact that, so far as her class is concerned, the primaeval laws still run"; and finally, the Deputation—two men and three women. "Superior people will call them Cranks. But Cranks have been of some service to the world, and the use of superior people is still to be discovered."[23]

The plot scarcely needs to be outlined after the characters have been established. Mrs. Chilvers, among the women, is the best candidate; the others, because of their extreme positions or attitudes are either less attractive or less capable. For example, Elizabeth Spender antagonizes with her superiority; Janet Blake lacks the necessary fire; Mrs. Montcalm Villiers is too self-centered. When all agree that Mrs. Chilvers presents the ideal women's candidate, the tension develops around the relationship between Mr. and Mrs. Chilvers as husband and wife. Intellectually, both accept the justice of the contested election; emotionally, they feel an imbalance growing. The question of their having no children brings a feeling of guilt never before voiced. As election activities increase, they become more estranged as Mrs. Chilvers enjoys the headiness of success and Mr. Chilvers becomes so disillusioned that he finally gives the order to his frustrated co-workers to go ahead with dirty politics.

Mrs. Chilvers wins. When she goes to the balcony to accept acclaim, Mr. Chilvers goes quietly home. When she later encounters him at home, he is charitably solving a problem for a mother of several children, one a boy who has done wrong. Mrs. Chilvers, who is unobserved, is so moved by pity and love for him, that she announces she is to become a mother; promises to give up politics for the time being—but only for the time being; and begs his continued effort for votes for women. He responds with the final speech of the play: "I thought you were drifting away from me: that strange voices were calling you away from life and motherhood. God has laughed at my fears. He has sent you back to me with His command. We will fashion His world together, we two lovers, Man and Woman, joined together in all things. It is His will. His chains are the children's hands" (167).

More than *Miss Hobbs*, the play is dated by its specifics relative to franchise for women. The general complaint in *Miss Hobbs* has been that woman's role in the home was degrading to her capabilities and dignity, a theme still relevant. A better-written play, *The Master of Mrs. Chilvers*, like most propaganda literature, loses relevance and force when the cause has been won. The over-all question still concerns the complementary nature of man's and woman's role in the family and society; the specific vehicle, the campaign for women's votes, remains a topic of a past decade.

The comedy hangs upon the personalities of the characters and the topical fun to be got out of the women's campaigning and the men's frustration between chivalry and competition.

Mr. Chilvers' role, in a sense the spokesman for the author, is that of a sober, understanding, enlightened gentleman who is in no way really comical. The situation in which he finds himself allows for irony when the enfranchisement which he has been championing in theory threatens in reality his own re-election. Furthermore, the contesting party includes not only his wife but a band of supporters headed by a somewhat formidable mother-in-law and by Phoebe, Annys' sister, of whom he is genuinely fond. The clash of Mr. Chilvers with Mrs. Spender provides not so much comedy as tension—dislike on both sides is couched in extreme courtesy that is equivalent to sarcasm.

Phoebe Mogton, Chilvers' sister-in-law, exhibits young enthusiasm as she cheers first one side, then the other, and is often happy about her brother-in-law's successes. Stage directions read, after one of her outbursts, *"She is not a quick thinker"* (31). Ginger provides the kind of role Jerome likes to have in both plays and stories; the cockney maid, brash, flip, funny. She has an understanding of the world—people's weaknesses—and she is good at heart. Furthermore, she likes a bit of flattery and the attentions of the men. Mrs. Chinn, "A Mother," has ten children. She is not interested in rights for women, and she thinks men are "probably doing their best, poor things!" (56); she, of course, is the antithesis of Mrs. Spender. When her boy is in trouble, she turns naturally to Mr. Chilvers, who is known for his compassion as well as his influence.

Annys Chilvers, like her husband, represents Jerome's ideal. Mentally alert, she sees the franchise movement as a means to a more ideal world. At the same time, she would like to be the ideal wife; and her relationships with Mr. Chilvers have made for a happy home until she runs for office. The speeches show her to be a person of charm as well as one with a will of her own. The difference between her point of view and that of Elizabeth Spender, champion of women's rights, appears from her questions and response to Mrs. Spender:

ANNYS: What do *you* understand is the true meaning of the woman's movement?

ELIZABETH: The dragging down of man from his position of supremacy. What else can it mean?
ANNYS: Something much better. The lifting up of woman to be his partner. (14)

The men of the cast provide counterparts to the women. Dorian St. Herbert, a lawyer who advises the women, enjoys the cause for the sake of the novelty, as does Mrs. Mountcalm Villiers. Hake, the butler, like Mrs. Chinn, is for the family; and he indicates the way some of the lower classes demonstrate equality for women by admitting that he sometimes sits with the children during his off hours so that Mrs. Hake may have an evening out. Jawbones, a comic character, knows how to cajole Ginger into a good humor. Slingsby and Lamb are the political aides to Mr. Chilvers: Lamb is a stuffy fellow-member of Parliament; Slingsby, the professional election manager, who also has a comic part.

The play contains a mixture of the comedy of the war between the sexes and Jerome's serious ideas. The changes between the serious and the comic are dramatically well-timed, and the characters are depicted with more individuality than Jerome has shown in previous works. Besides the contest for votes, the initial right of women to run for office turns out to be based on a House of Lords' reversal of a decision prohibiting a particular Irish lunatic to vote. "Mentally deficient" had included idiots, infants, and women; therefore, the Lords' decision had meant that "mentally deficient" women could vote. Almost all the Jeromian idealism appears in the play—the ideas that come to be the propaganda of his last two novels: his idea of love; his concern for humanity and the bringing about of a better future state.

The serious issues are presented in two ways—by Mrs. Chilvers' voiced aims and by an incident involving personal intervention out of pity. For example, Mrs. Chilvers, in thinking of what the vote for women will mean says: "Are not the children ours as well as yours? Shall we not work together to shape the world where they must dwell? Is it only the mothervoice that shall not be heard in your councils? Is it only the mother-hand that shall not help to guide? . . . It is to give, not to get—to mingle with the sterner judgments of men the deeper truth that God, through pain, has taught to women—to mingle with man's justice woman's pity, till there shall arise the perfect law—not made of man nor woman, but of both, each bringing what the other lacks" (23). However, when Mrs. Chinn seeks aid for her son, she goes not to Mrs. Chilvers but to Mr. Chilvers, who tries to make her see the moral issue, in terms, actually, of the women's statements:

GEOFFRY CHILVERS: You want me to tip the wink to the police to look the other way while you smuggle this young malefactor out of the clutches of the law?

MRS. CHINN: *(Quite indifferent to the moral aspect of the case)* If you would be so kind, sir.

GEOFFRY: Umph! I suppose you know what you're doing; appealing through your womanhood to man's weakness—employing "backstairs influence" to gain your private ends, indifferent to the higher issues of the public weal? All the things that are going to cease when woman has the vote. (157–58)

Mr. Chilvers does "tip the wink." Like Dickens, in *Hard Times*, Jerome apparently distrusts the courts and feels that setting aside the law because of compassion is justified; for this scene provides the climax that ends the play by bringing Annys Chilvers and Geoffrey Chilvers to an understanding.

VI The Passing of the Third Floor Back

The Passing of the Third Floor Back derives from a double source: Jerome's preoccupation with the dual nature of man, and his memory of a mysterious figure. Early in his career, when the young men Bernard Shaw, Arthur Conan Doyle, Philip Martston, A. C. Swinburne, and Jerome K. Jerome were journalist friends, the group was discussing the question of truth in autobiography. The Conclusion was that no man writes his true story: "It would be too painful. Society is built upon the assumption that we are all of us just as good as we should be. To confess that we are imperfect, is to proclaim ourselves unhuman." The group disbanded, but Philip Marston and Jerome continued the subject.[24] Marston, admitting that he *had* written the diary revealing his true self, confessed that he seemed to have a dual nature: "One Philip was an evil thing, full of lusts and horrors, lower than any beast that crawled the earth. And another Philip was quite beautiful, and Christ would have loved him. And, in addition to these two, was yet a third Philip, who stood apart from both. . . . He seemed to be always just behind the other two, watching them both with passionless eyes. 'There are times . . . when he looks into my very soul and I shrivel up with shame; and there are rare moments when I feel as if he had entered into me and we were one.' "[25] Marston's words match, in general, the ideas Jerome had already formed about man's basic nature; and they are the thesis of the play.

But an incident in Jerome's life crystalized the idea into a dramatic situation. Jerome recounts how the idea of the Stranger of *The Passing of the Third Floor Back* came to him: "I followed a stooping figure passing down a foggy street, pausing every now and then to glance up at a door. I did not see his face. It was his clothes that worried me. There was nothing out of the way about them. I could not make out why it was they seemed remarkable. I lost him at the corner, where the fog hung thick, and found myself wondering what he would have looked like if he had turned round and I had seen his face. I could not get him out of my mind, wandering about the winter streets; and gradually he grew out of those curious clothes of his."[26]

From Jerome's mysterious stranger, along with the conviction of the struggle between a person's evil and better self, *The Passing of the Third Floor Back* was born, first as a short story, then as a play. It was not an easy play to write. "One had to feel it rather than think it," but on its completion Jerome read it late one night to David Warfield and David Belasco at Belasco's theater in New York. "We had the house to ourselves; . . . It was about three o'clock in the morning, and the only thing we could get was cold beef and pickles. They were both impressed by the play, and we found ourselves talking in whispers. I fancy Belasco got nervous about it, later on. We fixed this up next morning . . . and he asked me to see Percy Anderson, the artist, when I got back to England, and get him to make sketches for the characters. It was while he was drawing them, in his studio at Folkestone, that one morning Forbes-Robertson . . . dropped in upon him.''[27] Forbes-Robertson played the part of the Stranger and it was, next to Hamlet, his most successful role; he played the part with dignity and compelling force. Jerome had originally written the part for David Warfield, who, Jerome thought, would have made the character win through tenderness and appeal. Nevertheless, the tremendous success of the play undoubtedly owed much to the skill of its prominent cast—"as perfect a cast as I think any play has ever had.''[28]

The subtitle of *The Passing of the Third Floor Back—, An Idle Fancy. In a Prologue, A Play, and an Epilogue*—indicates the three-act structure and hints at an imaginative interpretation. The cast of characters, like the cast of a modern morality play, in the Prologue appear solely as types: a Satyr, a Coward, a Bully, a Shrew, a Hussy, a Rogue, a Cat, a Cad, a Snob, a Cheat, a Passer-by. No such abstractions appear, however, in the realistic boardinghouse action of the Prologue. Instead, the reader (or playgoer) matches the type names to shrewish Mrs. Sharpe, the landlady; Stasia, the sluttish "slavey"; Joey Wright, the lecherous, retired bookmaker; Major Tompkins, retired and a cad; Mrs. Percival de Hooley, a snob—all of whom appear in action in the Prologue. Personal names are listed only before Part II, "The Play." At the beginning of "The Epilogue," personal names and types have been replaced by a new listing; and the type and specific names become general nomenclature: "The Lady of the House," "An Old Bachelor," "A Husband and Wife," "A Rich Aunt." Only the Stranger remains nameless; he appears first as "A Passerby," then specifically as "The Third Floor Back," and finally as "A Friend."

The Prologue opens at 13 Bloomsbury Square where, according to the short-story version, "the keeping of second-rate boarding houses . . . does not tend to develop the virtues of generosity and amiability.''[29] Mrs. Sharpe, the Landlady, who is obviously shrewish, exchanges caustic remarks with Stasia, in the course of which the two characterize the boarders before each appears and demonstrates that he or she is as petty, snobbish, cowardly, or selfish as his morality name suggests. The bickering over the newspaper, the diluting of the whisky, the listening at the keyhole, the snide remarks, and the broad jokes disclose a segment of society that has grown spiteful by allowing free rein to the meanest traits.

A simple plot emerges as Major and Mrs. Tompkins try to marry their daughter, Vivian, to old Joey Wright, an ex-bookmaker. Vivian, formerly attracted to artist Christopher Penny, seems not unwilling to marry Joey; for she covets wealth and the luxuries she knows Christopher cannot give her. Christopher Penny, discouraged by the rewards of his honest art, has already taken steps to compromise his ideals by agreeing to a proposal by the two commercialists, Jape Samuels and Harry Larkcom, to paint salacious pictures. To this group of people—including Mrs. Percival de Hooley, who continually intrudes her relationship to aristocracy, and Miss Kite, the old maid who tries to appear young—the Stranger, answering Stasia's notice of a vacant room, appears.

The boardinghouse guests, with each encounter with the Stranger, find themselves looking into their own hearts and not liking the traits found there—lust, petty vengeance, and belittling each other. By the end of the Prologue, the Landlady and Stasia have begun to change; they condemn their worser natures and do small positive acts of honesty or charity. Mrs. Sharpe reduces the price of the room to the Stranger to what it should be; and she allows Stasia, already struck by the new spirit introduced into the house, to take a half-hour off before dinner. New life in the boardinghouse has begun.

In the Play (Part II), the Stranger, the occupant of the third-floor back, encounters each boarder in turn. He convinces Major Tompkins that, as a gentleman, he really should show the courtesy and love for his wife that he formerly felt. The Stranger persists in acting as if the Major cannot conceal his love; he persuades Mrs. Tompkins that she has been fortunate in having married the Major and suggests that he, the Stranger, was once an admirer of hers in her earlier Devonshire days. The daughter, Vivian, tries unconvincingly to show the Stranger that she does not love the penniless painter and to deny that she cares only for money. The Stranger reminds Christopher Penny of his first art teacher who had prompted his ideals. The Stranger convinces Mr. Larkcom that he is a born entertainer and that there is joy in giving pleasure to others through songs and his other music-hall gifts.

To Jape Samuels, who is planning to rook Joey Wright of his money, the Stranger appeals and, by speaking to his racial pride, makes him reject his dishonest plans as something which would degrade him and his people. The stranger transforms the snobbish Mrs. de Hooley into a respected gentlewoman, the poor relative of aristocracy but a benefactor to her own poorer relatives. He persuades Miss Kite to leave off her paint and be the genuine, likeable middle-aged person she could be. Last of all, he causes Joey Wright to sacrifice the immediate power to purchase a young bride to the long-range benefit of becoming a benefactor to art. Joey promotes, then, the finer painting of Christopher Penny and becomes a genuine friend to the young couple. Each boarder finds himself searching for his better self and condemning his own malice as he comes face to face with the Stranger. Moreover, each also has a vague recollection of having known the Stranger before.

The Epilogue opens on the same boardinghouse scene, but the place has now become pleasant and homelike. *"Good taste, among other things, would seem to have entered into the house since last we saw it,"* read the stage directions. When a Friday afternoon open-house brings all boarders except the Stranger into the drawing room as guests, each character shows that he has been transformed. Each now lives his better self as the result of the brief encounter with "the third-floor back." Consideration for one another, honesty, and pride in their efforts to overcome weaknesses mark their behavior. The Stranger appears—at first only as a voice or as music heard; but he appears to Stasia and to Mrs. Sharpe in actuality, not as the Wanderer or Stranger, but as "A Friend." As each guest leaves, he too recognizes the Stranger and tells him of the reform in his own life. The Stranger then takes leave of Mrs. Sharpe, who promises always to have room for him. To Stasia, he speaks last, saying that he also must work, that he also is a servant, but that he came to her "because you wanted me." When he leaves, the face of Stasia, amidst the sunlight that has marked the Stranger's first entry to the boardinghouse, *"is the face of one to whom Love itself has spoken."*[30]

The idea of the mysterious supernatural visitor who effects changes in the lives of those he contacts appears a fairly constant theme in literature. The Stranger in this play, never identified as Christ, nevertheless makes his entry accompanied by increasing sunlight, the sound of music, or overtones of the Bible. Because of the subtitle *An Idle Fancy*, the play can be interpreted as the answer to the question, "What would happen if Christ were here?" That the Stranger appears to the shoddy, the foolish, and the fallen reinforces the message that Christ came to save not the righteous but the sinner. The power of Jerome's Stranger, however, operates solely as a catalyst, not a miracle; for the reformation of each character is accomplished by himself. Basically, each character proves to be good, and the faith which the Stranger has in each person's innate nobility serves to make each one determine to live his nobler self.

The pattern, in fact, of recognition, rejection, and the positive thrust forward establishes the structure of the play. Each character, beginning with Stasia and her employer, Mrs. Sharpe, recognizes the ugly nature that he has grown into. He becomes angry, not at the Stranger who persists in seeing the good in him, but at himself for what he now is. The former innocent, idealist, artist, kind woman, loving wife, or whatever turns on his or her base behavior, renounces it, and recaptures his earlier good self. Triggered by the Stranger's reaction to him, his direction in life changes.

The characters of the play break down into "They" and "He"; and, among the "they" of the boardinghouse in Bloomsbury Square, a fair cross-section of society appears: master and servant relationship with Stasia and Mrs. Sharpe; young lovers in Vivian and Christopher Penny (who are not in the short-story version); a married couple; an old bachelor and an old maid in Joey Wright and Miss Kite, respectively; a widow in Mrs. DeHooley; a young unscrupulous businessman in Larkcom; and a representative of a minority race in Samuels, the Jew.

Characters change from comic to tender in the course of
the action. Stasia, more than any other of the Bloomsbury re-
sidents, stands out with some individuality. She is cheeky,
slatternly, perhaps somewhat picaresque. In answer to Mrs.
Sharpe's repeated calling, she enters the play saying "All
right—all right. Don't shout. Spoil yer voice for singing,"
(8); and, in answer to the question as to what she has been
doing, she replies, "Injoring myself. All there is to do in this
place." Then she gleefully confesses that she had given to
old Joey Wright, who was somewhat fuddled with drink,
" 'alf a tumberful of cold tea and filled it up with soda water.
'E went to bed singing" (9). To Mrs. Sharpe's offer of a
blouse she has finished wearing, Stasia counters: "Rather
'ave it 'fore you've done with it, if ye're sure yer can spare it.
Don't want to be mistook when I go out, for a bit of old London" (10).

Jerome's touch with dialects is good; and Stasia, fore-
shadowing an Eliza Doolittle, emerges as a pert, comic
character who has zest and impudence, and whose tenderness cannot be labeled maudlin. [31] When, in defiance of Mrs.
Sharpe, Stasia places the vacancy sign in the window, she
reacts with a puzzled smile at the beam of sunlight that
enters: "Gorblimy, if it ain't the sun! Forgotten all about
'im!" (14) Later, when all have exhibited their petty selves,
Stasia prepares for the entry of the Stranger with her note of
despair: "What's the good of us all, that's what I want to
know? . . . What's the use of us? What's the good of us to
ourselves or to anybody else?" (50-51) Stasia exhibits no
particular fault to be eradicated, though from the Prologue
Mrs. Sharpe taunts her with being fresh from the Industrial School; and Larkcom seems to think her an easy mark.
Stasia nevertheless assumes more importance with the
Stranger than do the other characters. Quicker than the
others, she recognizes his power. She represents the lowest
class on the social scale but is the recipient of the Stranger's
most attention. He, too, is a servant, he explains; and the play
ends with Stasia alone on the stage, basking in the sunlight
of Love.

As a morality play, *The Passing of the Third Floor Back*
makes an appeal to the consciences of the audience. Its

appearance was in tune with a generation that found satisfaction in Jerome's message, even as today's audiences react to themes of psychoanalysis and social violence. The Stranger, a most difficult part, had to be kept from being maudlin or saccharine. Jerome in the short story wishes to show the Stranger at times as burdened and old with cares of the world, but at other times as vigorous and full of young manhood. On the stage this portrayal is a matter for the actor. Jerome could depict the "beggar-saint" better in the short story and in the similar characters he uses in the novels. For example, the minister in *All Roads Lead to Calvary* is the old man with the haunting eyes; but he becomes a young peasant in the war trenches at the end of the novel. In *Anthony John*, he is the legendary figure, "Wandering Peter," whom the poor folk know. In these works Jerome makes a convincing mystic character. In the play, the dialogue carries the burden; and Jerome is dependent entirely upon the actor.

As in most of Jerome's plays, the dialogue of *The Passing of the Third Floor Back* surprisingly does not have the sparkle of Jerome's dialogue in humorous essays, the "Idler" type of humor. In the play, it is often disappointingly commonplace. We can only surmise that Jerome's experience on the stage convinced him how much the performers contribute, and assume from the actual success of his plays on stage that the actors and audience do find the lines adequate in performance.

CHAPTER 5

The Idler as Novelist

JEROME K. Jerome began writing novels only after he
had won acclaim as a humorist, an editor, and a playwright. Somewhat at loose ends after the disastrous lawsuit
which had forced his selling his interest in *To-day* and *The
Idler* and somewhat at odds with life in the West End of
London, he retraced his rise from the Poplar area to Mayfair:
"I never cared for the West End: well-fed, well-dressed,
uninteresting. The East, with its narrow silent streets where
mystery lurks; its noisome thoroughfares, teeming with
varied life, became again my favourite haunt. . . . My
wanderings would lead me to the little drab house off the
Burdett Road, where 'Paul Kelver' lived in his childhood."[1]
Of all his books, Jerome liked writing *Paul Kelver* (1902)
the best, "Maybe because it was all about myself, and people
I had known and loved."[2] It changed his luck with the critics; for after Francis Gribble had praised it, other critics
did so. Though *Paul Kelver* received praise and its success
surprised Jerome, he turned back to playwriting. Then, in
1904, he wrote another novel, *Tommy and Co.*, a loosely
tied-together story in which Jerome records half-seriously
and half-comically the newspaper world he knew so well.
They and I, a novel published in 1909, humorously bridges
the generation gap in its theme.

With the tremendous popularity of his moral drama *The
Passing of the Third Floor Back* and the critical acclaim of
Paul Kelver, Jerome felt secure in the knowledge that he
could write seriously. No longer accepted only as a humorist,
he could now turn to "the world's cry of pain."[3] *All Roads
Lead to Calvary* (1919), written at the end of World War I,
more than any other work of Jerome's, confronts the prob-

lems of a protagonist and her problem as an independent woman, her personal idealism, her dream of society. *Anthony John,* the last of Jerome's four novels, returns to the Midlands of his birth and again, with autobiographical overtones, deals with wealth, poverty, and evil. It also becomes a vehicle for Jerome's religious idealism.

The novel form was congenial to Jerome. Jerome had skill in the dramatic arts, and he had ability to write good humor; but the novel, with its opportunity for character analysis through the author's comments, provides Jerome an ideal medium. In *Paul Kelver,* in *All Roads Lead to Calvary,* in *Anthony John,* and, to a lesser extent, in *Tommy and Co.,* Jerome could build from his own experiences a portrait of the young individual who struggles to establish his identity.

I   Paul Kelver *(1902)*

Paul Kelver opens with a fanciful conversation between the adult Paul and the old house in Poplar, East London— the house that knew the secrets of the family. The fictional Paul Kelver queries the house, seeking the truth about his parents' love for each other, about his own youthful dreams, his own fears. The house, grumbling, asks why, since Paul is now an author, he doesn't write a book about the "shy, awkward boy," about "the mother [who] had a good man, and your father a true wife," and about the doctor with "the ugliest mouth and the loveliest eyes" ever known in a man. Because of this hint, Paul writes—the story of "a very ordinary lad who lived with a very ordinary folk in a modern London street, and who grew up to be a very ordinary sort of man, loving a little and grieving a little, helping a few, struggling and failing and hoping . . ." (7).

Paul's earliest memories return to his beginnings in Devonshire where he, his mother, and her crabby sister "with the three corkscrew curls each side of her head" wait for the husband who is in London to send for them. When he does, Paul, the aunt, and his mother, who is eager to join her husband but sad to leave the Devonshire home, take the train to London. The "tall man in grey" swoops down upon them and carries them off to a house in the East End for which he angrily apologizes. Paul's mother pretends enchantment with the place, but the aunt smoothes the awkward reunion in her brusque manner: "Nonsense! . . . it's a poky hole, as I told her it would be. Let her thank the Lord she's got a man clever enough to get her out of it. I know him; he could never rest where he was put. Now he's at the bottom, he'll go up" (24). The idea reassures at the moment, but the Kelvers never do go very far up; indeed, Mr. Kelver once confides to Paul that he is one of the unlucky ones of the world. Though business affairs are better at times, the house in Poplar remains Paul's home until that sad year when his youth ends with the deaths of the three older members of the family.

To a child, however, poverty does not always appear as grim as to adults; and the family carefully retains its mark of gentility by the employment of a servant or, when they are absolutely destitute, by subterfuges of one kind or another which, to the boy, are like a game. Paul's first awareness of women comes on such an occasion when, the servant having left the Kelvers in the lurch, Barbara, the laughing, attractive daughter of Mr. Hasluck, a client of his father, and Paul substitute as parlor maid and footman, respectively. Paul notices for the first time Barbara's beauty, but he cannot quite grasp why Barbara, older than Paul, is petulant at the lack of attention from the male adults. He observes the uneasiness, even the rising jealousy, of his mother at the attention Mr. Kelver pays to Mrs. Teidelmann, the young wife of their guest.

The Kelvers are strict Nonconformists, and the mother is rigidly pious. For some time Paul finds himself torn between an uncomfortable devotion to his mother and the attraction of Mrs. Teidelmann. "Often my mother, talking to me would chill me with the vista of the life that lay before me: a narrow, viewless way between twin endless walls of 'Must' and 'Must not.' This soft-voiced lady set me dreaming of life as of sunny fields through which one wandered, laughing, along the winding path of Will; so that, although, as I have said, there lurked at the bottom of my thoughts a fear of her, yet something within me I seemed unable to control went out to her, drawn by her subtle sympathy and understanding of it" (102). An invitation to see a pantomime, *Dick Whitting-*

ton, brings the conflict to a dramatic moment; for Mrs. Kelver refuses Paul permission to go; and for the moment, anger alienates Paul from his mother. Later, Mrs. Teidelmann, about to leave for the Continent, sends for Mrs. Kelver, who takes Paul with her for the interview. Mrs. Teidelmann is ill. Waiting for her to awake, Mrs. Kelver hears words spoken in delirium that make Mrs. Kelver trust her— in fact, sympathize with her. She no longer questions her husband's fidelity,". . . and from that day my mother's whole manner changed. Not another angry word ever again escaped her lips, never an angry flash lighted up again her eyes" (107).

Dr. Hal Washburn, of the ugly mouth and beautiful eyes, the family physician and mentor to Paul, orders Mrs. Kelver to vacation for her health; so she and Paul return to Devonshire. Mrs. Kelver enjoys reminiscing, and they climb to old Jacob's Tower, where she can look down over scenes full of dear memories.

Suddenly she raised her head and listened. . . . and then from the woods came a faint, long-drawn "Coo-ee." We ran to the side of the tower commanding the pathway from the village and waited, until from among the dark pines my father emerged into the sunlight. Seeing us, he shouted again and waved his stick, and from the light of his eyes and his gallant bearing, and the spring of his step across the heathery turf, we knew instinctively that trouble had come upon him. He always rose to meet it with that look and air. It was the old Norse blood in his veins, I suppose. (110)

They learn that Mr. Kelver has broken with Mr. Hasluck, an irreplaceable client, largely because Mr. Kelver cannot tolerate Hasluck's dishonesty. In the scene that follows, Mrs. Kelver demonstrates her courage, especially when Mr. Kelver also reveals that his health is undermined by an old injury from the mines and that he has only a short time to live.

The eighteen months that follow are happy ones, for pettiness and worries are laid aside. "Again we lived poorly, but there was now no pitiful straining to keep up appearances, no haunting terror of what the neighbours might think" (118). Even Aunt Fan decides to "give amiability another trial," but the months seem so much shorter than they have planned that there is scarcely time enough to enjoy all they intend. One night, though, is given to an outing to the theater—the first attendance of any of the family at such a worldly entertainment. "We will all be wicked together," says Mrs. Kelver. When the three Kelvers and Barbara leave for a performance of "A Voice from the Grave, or the Power of Love—a New and original drama in five acts and thirteen tableaux,"

> Which of us was the most excited . . . it would be difficult to say. Barbara, feeling keenly her responsibility as prompter and leader of the dread enterprise, sat anxious, as she explained to us afterwards, hoping there would be nothing shocking in the play, nothing to belie its innocent title . . My father was the youngest of us all. Compared with him I was sober and contained. He fidgeted—people remarked upon it. He hummed. . . . Every minute he would lean across to inquire of my mother: "How are you feeling—all right?" To which my mother would reply with a nod and a smile. She sat very silent herself, clasping and unclasping her hands . . . . "It seems very orderly and—and respectable," whispered my mother. There seemed a touch of disappointment in her tone. (130–31)

But not all the memories of this period are happy ones. The failing health of his father forces early upon Paul the confrontation of his faith and his fears. At first, he cannot grasp the fact that his father is dying; and when comprehension comes suddenly, he races home from school, "the terror and the hurt of it" growing with every step. "I ran as if I feared he might be dead before I could reach the office. He was waiting for me with a smile as usual, and I flung myself sobbing into his arms" (136). The father understands and comforts him. "It might have come to us earlier, my dear boy," he would say, with his arm round me, "or it might have been a little later. . . . I cannot think that He will let us die; and that we're to think of Him as without purpose. But His uses may not be our desires. . . . 'Though He slay me, yet will I trust in him.' . . . I looked up into my father's face, and the peace that shone from it slid into my soul and gave me strength" (138).

Sooner than the family has expected, the father dies. His aunt, too, complaining that she would never be missed, "died as she had lived, grumbling" (159). Paul discovers as his mother, too, grows weaker in health, that his father's investments have been in the hands of an embezzler. He manages to keep the news from her so that she is more at peace in her illness; but upon her death, Paul is not only emotionally but literally bankrupt.

For Paul, a dreary period of boardinghouse existence ensues. His schooling which consists of a few years as a day-pupil at an academy where, but for the friendship of one boy, Dan, he would have been unbearably lonely, has prepared him for a clerkship; and Paul finally secures the position of purchasing clerk for an East India Company broker. Paul's childhood mentor, Dr. Hal, has advised him to "Put your Carlyle in your pocket; he is not all voices, but he is the best maker of men I know" (185). Now, as he passes through a Center of Indifference, Paul finds his Carlyle useful: "Reduce your denominator—you know the quotation. I found it no philosophical cant, but a practical solution of life" (195). However, it is the emotional rather than the material hardship that he finds difficult to endure:

I was alone. I knew not a living soul to whom I dared to speak who cared to speak to me. For those first twelve months after my mother's death I lived alone, thought alone, felt alone. In the morning, during the busy day, it was possible to bear; but in the evenings the sense of desolation gripped me like a physical pain. . . . I would walk into the parks and, sitting there, watch with hungry eyes the men and women, boys and girls, moving all around me, talking, laughing, interested in one another; feeling myself some speechless ghost, seeing but not seen, crying to the living with a voice they heard not. . . . For company I mingled with ragged men, frowsy women, ageless youths, gathered round the red glow of some coffee-stall.

Rarely would we speak to one another. More like animals we browsed there, sipping the halfpenny cup of hot water coloured with coffee-grounds . . . munching the moist slab of coarse cake; looking with dull, indifferent eyes each upon the wretchedness of the others. Perhaps some two would whisper to one another in list-less, monotonous tone, broken here and there by a short mirthless laugh; some shivering creature, not yet case-hardened to despair, seek, perhaps, the relief of curses that none heeded. Later, a faint chill breeze would shake the shadows loose, a thin wan light streak the dark air with shade, and silently, stealthily, we would fade away and disappear. (196 and 199)

To assuage the loneliness, Paul begins writing—not in the humorous style which had amused his school friend, not about the London "with its million characters, grave and gay . . . its pathos, and its humour [which] lay to my hand," but about cottage maidens, bucolic yeomen "among mountains, or in moated granges" (200). He tastes the thrill of publication, and he finally makes friends in a lodging house presided over by Mrs. Peedles, a sometime actress in Charles Kean's company. A comic involvement after a convivial boardinghouse party leaves Paul engaged to Miss Sellars, who is totally unsuited to him. He tries to be honorable; but with the aid of the boardinghouse sympathizers, Mr. Jarman, Minikin, the O'Kelly, and Mrs. Peedles, he escapes from the entanglement by taking to the road under an assumed name with a traveling company of actors.

Paul proves no great actor since his weak voice is a drawback; but beginning with bit parts, he is tolerated and commences his career with anticipation. "On the first night, passing the gallery entrance on my way to the stage door, the sight of the huge crowd assembled there waiting gave me my first taste of artistic joy. I was a part of what they had come to see, to praise or to condemn, to hear, to watch. Within the theatre there was an atmosphere of suppressed excitement, amounting almost to hysteria" (265). On this first night, the leading lady, seeing the sparks in his eyes advises, "Get out of this life if you can. It's bad for a woman; it's still worse for a man. To you especially it will be harmful." "Why to me in particular?" "Because you are an exceedingly foolish little boy," she answers with another laugh, "and rather nice" (226). But it takes more than advice to make Paul realize the truth, and he continues with the company, playing varied parts, sometimes writing and revising the plays.

After one performance he encounters his school friend, Dan, who has become a moderately successful young journalist due largely to brashness and luck. They decide to take rooms in the house of the once-popular pre-Raphaelite painter Deleglise and to share housekeeping duties and to continue their careers. Paul is already dreaming of becoming a second Kean or of taking Macready's place. When Dan encourages him to write, Paul feels he "could combine the two: fill Drury Lane in the evening, turn out epochmaking novels in the morning, write [his] own plays" (278). His optimism rises, too, when he encounters the daughter of Deleglise, a bit of a hoyden, younger than he. She is practicing grown-up courtesy when he surprises her in her father' studio. Indignant at his intrusion, she slaps him. "I sprang at her, and catching her before she had recovered her equilibrium, kissed her. I did not kiss her because I wanted to. I kissed her because I could not box her ears back in return. . . . I kissed her, hoping it would make her mad. It did" (285).

And so, a frank, merry friendship grows up between Paul and Norah Deleglise. Friendship with Norah brings to mind his adolescent adoration of Barbara Hasluck of the old Poplar-house days. He hunts up Mr. Hasluck and finds Barbara also at home. She is preparing for marriage with a Spanish nobleman, and she lets Paul know that she deeply loves and is loved by another. Paul is shocked to learn that it is his childhood guide, Dr. Hal Washburn, whom she really loves. Paul, himself, does not wish to marry Barbara, as she has always been to him a "vision of my dream. . . . I knew that when next I saw her there would be a gulf between us I had no wish to bridge. To worship her from afar was a sweeter thought to me than would have been the hope of a passionate embrace. To live with her, sit opposite to her while she ate and drank, see her, perhaps, with her hair in curl-papers, know possibly that she had a corn upon her foot . . . would have been torture to me. . . . She would marry. The thought gave me no pain" (295–96). Nevertheless, the cynicism of the whole affair disturbs Paul.

His idealism receives a second shock when he is encouraged by Urban Vane, a well-known writer whom he has met in Deleglise's studio, to share in a stage production with him—to revamp a play. Paul's name is to appear as author. Against the advice of Dan and Norah, who with her "Dreams

are silly," and "You are not really awake yet," (324) angers
him, he leaves London, triumphant in his vanity. A year later
he sneaks back, defeated, disgraced; for the play which he
has been producing and has "adapted" had been stolen by
Urban Vane, who thought the author, dying in Italy, would
not know. The real author has survived, rumors become ugly,
and Paul discovers the duplicity of his partner who decamps,
leaving Paul with both the shame and the financial load. He
cannot pay his actors.

Frightened and humiliated, he leaves the theater on tour
in Ireland, walks thirty miles to Belfast, and spends his last
pound getting back to London. There he takes lodgings, eking
out a bare living by giving lessons to shoeboys, and making
up tradesmen's books. He falls ill, hopes he will die, but
finds hunger driving him into the streets again. One early
morning he awakes from having slept the night on a park
bench to find Norah Deleglise beside him. When he confesses his whole miserable story to her, she laughs, hands
him a handkerchief for his tears, and convinces him that he
has needed the comedown. Norah is severe with him, however, about his paying the debts—a good hundred and fifty
pounds. She refuses to shake hands with him until he has
paid the last penny he owes, but she cheers him by stating
that the abused Italian author knew of Urban Vane's deceit
and has not blamed Paul.

It takes Paul three years to win the handshake that Norah
has refused—three years in which he works at "penny-a-
lining"; but he recaptures his sense of humor and puts it in
his writing, for, "seated at my rickety table, I laughed as I
wrote, the fourth wall of the dismal room fading before my
eyes, revealing vistas beyond" (361). Scenes witnessed from
his lonely walks around London, the teeming underworld
of the city, and the shabby life of the traveling actors appear
photographically to him; and his name and fame rise in
journalistic circles. The three years also provide comparisons
between the dream-vision of his Barbara and the helpmeet
affection of Norah. The Barbara who remains an object of
worship is, however, a memory of the past. Paul learns of
her from Dr. Hal himself, whom he encounters ill in a room
in Switzerland.

Dr. Hal's affair with Barbara has been a sordid one, for Barbara had left the Spanish Count to live with Dr. Hal. The Count does not apply for a divorce. Dr. Hal tells Paul, "She loved me well enough, but she loved the world also. . . . I watched her grow more listless, more depressed. . . . There was no bond between us except our passion. . . . We fell to mutual recriminations, vulgar scenes'" (304–05). After the Count and Dr. Hal meet and agree that Barbara may go back to the Count, Dr. Hal quietly dies. Then, unexpectedly, the Count sues for divorce and three years later, Paul encounters Barbara acting in a theatrical company and now married to a German Baron. When Paul visits her backstage, she gives him a ring he recognizes; it is from " 'a girl called Barbara. . . . She died, poor girl, three years ago.' . . . From under her painted lashes she flashed a glance at me. I hope never to see again that look upon a woman's face" (380).

Paul returns from the Continent to find his first comic opera a success and to learn that the painter Deleglise has died. He hurries to find Norah, who has continued to keep her father's house, where they met. She has seen Paul restore his faith in himself. Congratulating him on his comic opera, she counters his laments that his comic work falls short of his ambition to alleviate the world's cry of pain with the statement that his "fortress of laughter" may be a rallying-point for the forces of joy and gladness. With the recognition that Norah always has the word to help him and that he needs her support, Paul joins hands with Norah in a propsal of marriage.

The plot of *Paul Kelver* has been given at some length (1) because *Paul Kelver* is autobiographical, (2) because it is the best of his novels, and (3) because it treats the themes that recur in Jerome's work. Though autobiographical, *Paul Kelver* covers the years of the protagonist from early memories only to young success and prospective marriage. The formative period of life in the pattern of *David Copperfield* structures the novel. The debt to Charles Dickens is perhaps acknowledged in the scene in Victoria Park where the child Paul encounters the stranger on the park bench. When the stranger queries the boy on his literary ambitions and

draws him to talk of Dickens, Paul confesses an admiration
of Pickwick, only to elicit the response "Oh, damn Mr. Pickwick!" (155). The incident, which actually occurred to
Jerome with a stranger who must have been Dickens, acquires significance both in Jerome's thinking and in Paul's;
for the success of the humor that Jerome and Paul wrote
seemed to them trivial in comparison to their serious work.[4]

Jerome has divided *Paul Kelver* into two parts and a prologue, and the first book ends with the death of Paul's
mother. This first part as autobiography differs in minor
details from Jerome's own life, but the changes simplify and
focus attention upon relationships, influences, the formation
of the protagonist's character. The persons who emerge from
this part form a nucleus—father, mother, aunt, the family
doctor and friend, Dr. Hal, the wealthy client, Mr. Hasluck,
with his beautiful daughter Barbara, and the lightly sketched
school friend, Dan—all of whom spend a dozen years in the
Poplar district of the East End of London. That Jerome's
own family consisted of two older sisters and an older
brother who had died at the age of six, that he spent country
vacations with the married sister, and that the family did not
remain in the one house can be regarded as immaterial.
Autobiographical elements do concern the personalities of
his parents; his mother's influence in teaching him Welsh
romances and fairy stories; his father's unlucky nature; the
piety of both the parents and the Nonconformist atmosphere of the home; and most of all, the response of a sensitive boy to the action, the ideas, the people in this age, this
place.

Part two takes Paul at the age of fourteen, orphaned, without money, into the working world of London, where, like
Jerome himself, he works at meanly paid clerkships, battles
loneliness and hunger, but fortifies himself with a Carlylean
respect for work and duty. Like Jerome, Paul tries the theater
and then moves into journalism. He renews connections with
Dan, with Dr. Hal and Barbara; and with expanding friendship and success, he joins the Bohemian world of London.

Part two of *Paul Kelver* may have appeared as a *roman à
clef* to readers at the turn of the century. Whether or not the
characters are identifiable, they convince by their similarity

to the accounts given in memoirs and other reports of the period. Certain of the humorous bits are close to Jerome's journalistic reportage and sketching in other works. To readers of Jerome's *My Life and Times*, his autobiography published in 1926, characters such as Dan, the journalistic friend with whom Paul Kelver sets up housekeeping in the painter Deleglise's home, can be compositively identified. Jerome's father had two nephew doctors whom the boy visited and admired who are possible models for Dr. Hal. Paul's job with a commission agent for India corresponds with Jerome's first job, the stage experiences can be verified, and perhaps the lawyer art collector for whom Jerome worked supplies the model for the artist Deleglise.

The circle of Philip Marston, the blind poet, to which Jerome belonged, doubtless furnished the models for some of the Bohemian setting. Jerome's lodgings in Nelson Square on the other side of Blackfriar's Bridge were owned by a former actress. The name "Mrs. Peedles," the landlady of Paul's boardinghouse, is the name of the landlady of Tavistock Place where Jerome and George Wingrave shared lodgings. The house in Poplar and the Deleglise house in Queen Square can perhaps be identified. Jerome has a strong sense of place; for like the reader of a Dickens' novel, we can go from section to section of the London mentioned in *Paul Kelver*, sure that the streets are accurately named and placed in the fiction. But any writer putting his own life into his novel has the advantage of a schizophrenia that permits truthfulness when useful—and artistic license when needed.

Paul Kelver comes to the reader as a novel, and it must be judged as such. What remains poignant about the association between Jerome's life and that of his protagonist is the idealization, for example, in the novel of the family scene at the theater. In the words of Paul Kelver, "It happened to me before that very same curtain that many years later I myself stepped forth to make my first bow as a playwright. I saw the house but dimly. . . . All that I clearly saw was in the front row of the second circle—a sweet face laughing, though the tears were in her eyes. . . and on one side of her stood a gallant gentleman with merry eyes, who shouted 'Bravo!'

and on the other a dreamy-looking lad, but he appeared disappointed, having expected better work from me" (134). From *My Life and Times* we learn that the sister Blandina and Jerome shared the thrill of the theater, for the mother could not bring herself to approve it; and "the gallant gentleman with the merry eyes" had died before the brother and sister had had their first taste of the theater.

The novel, however, by itself merits attention for its story and for the skill with which it unfolds. Although the story progresses chronologically and divides into two parts, the novel has another structural framework that gives artistry to the work. Chapter headings form a continuous "Paul's Progress" in language that echoes the allegory of John Bunyan's *Pilgrim's Progress*. In terms of the journey, Paul "Arrives in a Strange Land, Learns Many Things, and Goes to Meet the Man in Grey." He "is Shipwrecked and Cast into Deep Waters." Chapter 1, Book II, is entitled "Describes the Desert Island to which Paul Was Drifted." He learns in Chapter VI "Of the Glory and the Goodness and the Evil that Go to the Making of Love." In another Chapter title, he "Sets Forth upon a Quest"; and, in the heading to the final chapter, Paul "Finds his Way." The archaic wording occurs only in the title headings. Nevertheless, such indicators at the heads of the chapters serve to link the action into a pattern revered by Nonconformists and familiar to English readers of life as a journey beset by temptations. Within the novel, the pattern of imagery is occasionally confirmed, as when Paul, restored in his own sight and in the opinion of others, seeks Dan. Dan remarks, "I left you alone. You had to go through it, your slough of despond. It lies across every path—that leads to anywhere" (376).

Another structural pattern which merges with the terms of Christian allegory gives meaning to the novel. Paul's earliest memories begin with his mother, who is of Welsh stock and who talks to him in the twilight evenings of "good men and noble women, ogres, fairies, saints and demons" (17). Myths and legends—"I took no harm from them, good rather, I think" (18). Upon arrival in Poplar, Paul is convinced that "London . . . was a city of the gnomes who labour sadly all their lives, imprisoned underground;

and a terror seized me lest I, too, should remain chained here, deep down below the fairy city that was already but a dream" (23). The imagery from fairyland and medieval romance which runs through the novel emphasizes life as a battle against the powers of evil and magic; and the images interweave with those suggesting the Christian pilgrimage. For example, Paul's first journey by train from Devonshire to London produces the monotonous chant of the rails to the little boy: "Here we suffer grief and pain,/ Here we meet to part again,' followed by a low, rumbling laugh; . . . still to this day the iron wheels sing to me that same song" (21). But a few minutes later, falling asleep, Paul "dreamed that as the result of my having engaged in single combat with a dragon, the dragon, ignoring all the rules of fairyland, had swallowed me" (22).

Later on, Paul refers to the money which Mr. Hasluck brings to them as "fairy gold." In his boyhood dreams Paul is "the comrade of a hundred heroes—I, who nightly rode with Richard Coeur de Lion, who against Sir Lancelot himself had couched a lance" (51); his meeting with Barbara Hasluck is "as though the fairy tales had all come true"; popularity at school becomes a knightly contest; and Paul encourages his father immensely by telling him that his mother has called her husband "our prince, fighting to deliver us from the grim castle called 'Hard Times,' guarded by the dragon Poverty" (39). Paul's love for Barbara always remains on the level of the medieval code of love; for Paul worships his avowed queen, not thinking of her in terms of marriage. There are many knightly references, but perhaps the blending of the knightly and the Christian can best be illustrated by Paul's thoughts when he discovers that he has been duped into a dishonest scheme that has deceived the theatergoing public and has cheated the actors:

I had been ambitious—I had been eager to make a name, a position for myself. But were I to claim no higher aim, I should be doing injustice to my blood—to the great-souled gentleman whose whole life had been an ode to honour, to her of simple faith who had known no other prayer to teach me than the childish cry, "God help me to be good!" I had wished to be a great man, but it was to have been a great good man. . . . I was to have been the knight without fear, but, rarer yet, without reproach—Galahad, not Lancelot. I had learned myself to be a feeble, backboneless fighter, conquered by the first serious assault of evil, a creature of mean fears, slave to every crack of the devil's whip, a feeder with swine. (344)

Still another division of the book occurs, the one in the psyche of Paul:

It was one of those hushed summer evenings when the air even of grim cities is full of whispering voices, and as, turning away from the river, I passed through the white toll-gate, I had a sense of leaving myself behind me on the bridge. So vivid was the impression that I looked back, half expecting to see myself still leaning over the iron parapet, looking down into the sunlit water. . . . The little chap never came back to me. He passed away from me as a man's body may possibly pass away from him, leaving only remembrance and regret. For a time I tried to play his games, to dream his dreams, but the substance was wanting. I was only a thin ghost, making believe. (59)

Late in the story, when Norah Deleglise sees Paul foolishly leaving with Urban Vane to become famous, she remarks that Paul lives in a dream. He laughs; then, "A flash of memory recalled to me that summer evening, upon Barking Bridge . . . . Was my boyhood in like manner falling from me" (343)? Reluctant as he is to admit it, he is leaving his youth behind him; the catastrophic experience with Urban Vane, in which he falls in his own esteem, provides the leap forward into maturity. The psychological division of the book corresponds with the chronological progress, but the divisions do not occur simultaneously—one division is determined by external events; the other, by interior development.

The main characters of the novel can be divided into three groups whose approach to life helps to initiate Paul into the world. They are his parents; Dr. Hal and Barbara; and Dan and Norah Deleglise. His father and mother represent an uncompromising idealism, which has its own strength but fails in the practical world. Dr. Hal and Barbara represent those who, recognizing ideals, sacrifice them cynically for material, selfish gain. Dan and Norah Deleglise have idealism but do not let it blind them to the means of functioning successfully in the material world.

Paul's parents express a love for each other that is deep, full of tenderness, sometimes foolish when they forget their poverty and pretend to wealth and dream of better times. "Children," is the term that the old house uses to describe them in the Prologue. Paul early decides that, if he were to describe a husband, he would call him "a man who could never rest quite content unless his wife were by his side, who twenty times a day would call from his office door, 'Maggie, are you doing anything important? I want to talk to you'. . . . Of a wife I should have said she was a woman whose eyes were ever love-lit when resting on her man, who was glad when he was and troubled when he was not" (27). When the shadow of jealousy comes between them, it is not permanent.

The failure of the parents lies in the father's "unluckiness"—as he calls it. An impractical man, he establishes himself in an area practicing law where, he later admits, only a criminal lawyer might gather a cliéntele. Hasluck comes to him for business, but Paul's father breaks with him over ethics; and Paul admits to himself that trying to regard Mr. Hasluck as a modern Robin Hood could not be done. Of his father, Paul says, "When [our fortunes] were dark again he was full of fresh hope, planning, scheming, dreaming again. It was never acting. A worse actor never trod this stage on which we fret. His occasional attempts at a cheerfulness he did not feel inevitably resulted in our all three crying in each other's arms. No, it was when things were going well that experience came to his injury" (83).

The Nonconformist faith of Paul's parents is as uncompromising as their idealism. Perhaps the comment Paul makes as he recalls the family's daring visit to the theater summarizes as well as Jerome ever does his feelings and Paul's toward Puritanism:

They had been bred in a narrow creed, both my father and my mother. That Puritan blood flowed in their veins that throughout our land has drowned much harmless joyousness; yet those who

know of it only from hearsay do foolishly to speak but ill of it. If
ever earnest times should come again, not how to enjoy but how to
live being the question, Fate demanding of us to show not what we
have, but what we are, we may regret that they are fewer among us
than formerly, those who trained themselves to despise all pleasure, because in pleasure they saw the subtlest foe to principle and
duty. No graceful growth, this Puritanism, for its roots are in the
hard, stern facts of life; but it is strong, and from it has sprung all
that is worth preserving in the Anglo-Saxon character. Its men
feared and its women loved God, and if their words were harsh
their hearts were tender. If they shut out the sunshine from their
lives, it was that their eyes might see better the glory lying beyond. . . . (129-30)

His mother "who had known no other prayer to teach me
than 'God help me to be good'" and his "great-souled
father whose whole life had been an ode to honour" (344)
remain an ideal for Paul.
    Dr. Hal Washburn and Barbara Hasluck, on the other
hand, recognize the forces of both good and evil in their
lives; and weighing virtue with personal gain, they opt for
personal gain. Deeply in love with Dr. Hal, Barbara will not
share his career among the poor. Having married the Count
for his title and social position, she then abandons marriage
for a love affair with Dr. Hal. "There was no bond between
us except our passion," the doctor explains. "The sordid, con-
temptible side of life became important to us. . . . Love
does not change the palate, give you a taste for cheap- claret"
(305). When their love affair fails, each goes his self-de-
structive way. So the compromise made to the world by two
he has admired hurts the idealistic Paul, who loves them both.
    Dan, the journalist friend, and Norah Deleglise seem
successfully to retain idealism and yet to be practical enough
in the workaday world. Dr. Hal had argued long on the differences between men's needs in love and women's. Dan,
on the other hand, in discussing Norah, whom he idolizes
but recognizes that she loves Paul, remarks that "The difference between men and women is very slight; we exag-
gerate for the purposes of art" (378). Norah's ideal, he explains, will be "a nice enough fellow—clever, but someone—
well, someone who will want looking after . . . who will

appeal to the mother side of her—not her ideal man, but the man for whom nature intended her" (378). When Paul recognizes the innuendos and suggests that, with the girl's help, he might in time become her ideal, Dan grumbles something about a long road ahead. The prospect of marriage brings the reader full circle to the relationship of Paul's parents to each other, but with the assurance that Norah can capably manage and that the new Paul, wiser from experience, can cope with the material world as his father could not.

The novel, in addition to the themes of love and religion, deals with poverty—as Paul faces it genteelly in his own family, as Dr. Hal faces it brutally and tenderly as a doctor in a slum area, and as Paul encounters it in the world of London clerks. The portrayal of Dr. Hal among the poor, whom he bullies at times and compassionately heals at others, is one of the effective parts of the book. Paul's childhood experiences outside the family circle are poignantly portrayed as the boy experiences the terror of the streets, the "anguish of the poor little beggar. . . . Gibes and jeers that after all break no bones. A few pinches, kicks, and slaps; at worst a few hard knocks. But the dreading of it beforehand! Terror lived in every street, hid, waiting for me, round each corner. The boy whistling . . . would I get past him without his noticing me, or would he . . . raise the shrill whoop that brought them from every doorway to hunt me" (51)? As a young man, beginning his way, he joins the corps of young clerks living in "third-floor back" rooms: "God rest you, gallant gentleman," he reflects, "lonely and friendless and despised; making the best of joyless lives; keeping yourselves genteel on twelve, fifteen, or eighteen (ah, but you are plutocrats!) shillings a week. May nothing you dismay. . . . Bullied and badgered and baited from nine to six though you may be, from then till bed time you are rorty young dogs" (184).

The "rorty young dogs" do represent another phase of the novel, for *Paul Kelver* is by no means all seriousness or pathos. There is an irrepressible sense of humor all the way through, particularly in Part II. The companions of the second part of the book form two groups, the London journa-

lists and the boardinghouse company that is primarily connected with the theater. These minor characters do not
appear with the convincing realism of the major characters.
Still, some of the personalities are effective. Jarman, for
example, of the Peedles' boardinghouse comes to life better
than a similar character in Jerome's *The Passing of the Third
Floor Back;* and Jarman is introduced thus:

> Our second-floor front was a young fellow in the commercial line.
> Jarman was Young London personified—blatant, yet kind-hearted;
> aggressively self-assertive, generous to a fault; cunning, yet at the
> same time frank; shrewd, cheery, and full of pluck. "Never say
> die" was his motto, and anything less dead it would be difficult to
> imagine. All day long he was noisy, and all night long he snored.
> He woke with a start, bathed like a porpoise, sang while dressing,
> roared for his boots, and whistled during his breakfast. His en-
> trance and exit were always to an orchestration of banging doors,
> directions concerning his meals shouted at the top of his voice as
> he plunged up or down the stairs, the clattering and rattling of
> brooms and pails flying before his feet. His departure always left
> behind it the suggestion that the house was now to let. (209)

Friendly to Paul, he encourages Paul's literary ambitions in
his own way:

> "You fire away, Shakespeare Redivivus. . . . Don't delay the
> tragedy. Why should London wait? I'll keep quiet."
>   But his notion of keeping quiet was to retire into a corner and
> there amuse himself by enacting a tragedy of his own in a hoarse
> whisper, accompanied by appropriate gesture.
>   "Ah, ah!" I would hear him muttering to himself, "I've killed
> 'er good old father; I 'ave falsely accused 'er young man of all the
> crimes that I 'ave myself committed. . . . It is streeange!" Then
> changing his bass to a shrill falsetto: "It is a cold and dismal night;
> the snow falls fast. . . . (209-10)

Jarman expresses young man-about-town opinions about
love as well. The misguided romance between Paul and the
Lady 'Ortensia adds life. Amusing enough, it never forms a
part of the serious discussions on love and marriage. On the
other hand, neither are the boardinghouse scenes nor those
among the actors quite as separated from the main characters

as are some of the sketches of a Dickens novel; for all contribute to Paul's life experience. The O'Kellys, Jarman, Mrs. Peedles, Urban Vane, are not grotesques; and Paul, tempted to be ashamed of his boardinghouse friends, receives Dan's rebuke of "an ounce of originality is worth a ton of convention. Little tin ladies and gentlemen all made to pattern! One can find them everywhere. Your friends would be an acquisition to any society" (316).

The novel contains several vignettes—a quick sketch, for example, of lawyer Stillwood's wife, virtually purchased as a child by the man to be educated and then presented as his bride ten years later. The pictures bear the stamp of truth, and we are certain they derive from Jerome's world of observation, though they convincingly fit into Paul's journey as well.

As for the language of *Paul Kelver*, Jerome has the ear for detecting characteristic speech, whether it be family expressions, London hoodlum speech, or the language of traveling actors in offstage hours. One example from the family scene illustrates this capability. Paul, given a half-crown for spending by Mr. Hasluck at a time when the family is particulary poor, still is urged to spend it as he likes. Long hours of indecision, of asking advice, and of contemplating shop windows finally produce his own decision to buy a dozen squares of colored glass, used chiefly for lavatory doors and staircase windows: "Why I bought them I did not know at the time, and I do not know now. My mother cried when she saw them. My father could get no further than, 'But what are you going to do with them?' to which I was unable to reply. My aunt alone attempted comfort. 'If a person fancies coloured glass,' said my aunt, 'then he's a fool not to buy coloured glass when he gets the chance. We haven't all the same tastes'" (45).

Paul Kelver remains a fine novel, universal enough to survive the times. Like Samuel Butler's posthumous *The Way of All Flesh* (which appeared in 1903, a year later than Jerome's novel) and Edmond Gosse's autobiography, *Father and Son* (1907), *Paul Kelver* gives a picture of a young man reared in a strict Evangelical home. Unlike these two bitter accounts of Victorian piety, Jerome's hero is tolerant, nonvindictive. *Paul Kelver* engrosses the reader. Most contemporary reviewers wrote enthusiastically of it. The novel deserves more attention today and at least a reprinting of it to make it available. In spite of its success, copies of *Paul Kelver* are difficult to find.

II   Tommy and Co. *(1904)*

In *My Life and Times,* Jerome K. Jerome tells of a childhood encounter with a woman to whom he confided that he was writing a book in which he would be the hero. "There is only one person you will ever know," she told me. "Always write about him. You can call him, of course, different names" (27). Jerome did not forget the advice, for *Tommy and Co.* grows out of Jerome's journalistic experiences. A much slighter novel than *Paul Kelver,* it pictures a group at least similar to "Jerome's young men." The novel, not chronologically developed by a first-person narrator as was *Paul Kelver,* depends upon the intriguing gamin "Tommy" for the unifying element in what in some respects is a related group of short stories. How the street waif, Tommy, scarcely knowing whether she is boy or girl, comes to Peter Hope, hack journalist, initiates the action. Ancillary stories bring in new characters. Before their stories are completed, the characters converge upon Peter Hope and Tommy for solutions to their problems, until from the group a managing director, a publisher, and a staff emerge for the founding of *Good Humour,* a paper with Peter Hope as editor and with Tommy the sub-editor. Subsequent stories concern private problems of the staff, solved or observed by the group, or the pranks that they play on each other. By the last story, seven years have elapsed; and Tommy, now of marriageable age, faces her own serious love complication.

The table of contents establishes the structure of the novel with chapter headings that describe the making of a newspaper staff: "Peter Hope Plans his Prospectus," "William Clodd Appoints Himself Managing Director," "Grindly Junior Drops into the Position of Publisher," "Miss Ramsbotham Gives Her Services," "Joey Loveredge Agrees—on certain terms—to Join the Company," "'The Babe' Applies for Shares," "Dick Danvers Presents His Petition." Yet,

each chapter is headed within the book as "Story the First,"
etc., and each of the seven chapters could be read separately
as a short story. In the first story, Peter Hope and Tommy find each other;
Tommy the waif is looking for a shelter, and she thinks
Peter Hope a "soft touch" from what she has overheard at
the café. Peter Hope, a widower for some years, feels a
strange attraction to the twelve-year-old, as "it" reminds
him of his own little Tommy, buried with his mother.
Tommy, unsuccessfully renamed "Jane," is touchingly
funny with her impish ways and a pride all her own. An
abominable cook, she becomes offended by Peter's attempts
to eat at the club. He hits upon the expedient of promoting
Tommy to the then-imaginary position of editorial assistant.
Liking the rewrite work which she does for him, she listens
avidly as Peter and other journalists talk. When they grumble
over the difficulty of getting an interview with the visiting
prince, she secretly undertakes the task. With her street-
urchin knowledge, she gets access to the prince's private
railroad car and surprises the prince and everyone else with
her exclusive interview, a real journalistic scoop.

The second story originates in the neighborhood of Gough
Street where Peter Hope and Tommy live, but it concerns
Mrs. Postwhistle's problem with a lodger who imagines from
week to week that he is a different animal species. She confides her uneasiness to William Clodd, rent collector,
"twenty-three and a born hustler," who, scenting money,
offers to take care of the lodger and does so. Eventually, upon
the death of his charge, Clodd confounds the heartless relatives with a choice of two wills: one of which leaves them
some money and to William Clodd, "as a return for the many
kindnesses shown him" the residue of the estate, about
eleven hundred pounds; the alternative will leaves all the
money to the Royal Zoological Society. With the money,
William Clodd, Esquire, proposes to be the proprietor of a
newspaper to be edited by Peter Hope, assisted by Miss
Jane Hope.

The third story shows how Grindley Junior wins the love
of Helvetia Appleyard. They are a young couple affianced as
children by their Jewish parents who have quarreled since

Grindley Senior has become the wealthy producer of Grindley's Sauce. When Grindley Junior disappoints his father by his failures at the university, Grindley Senior sends the young man to learn the grocery business from the ground up— that is, from Mrs. Postwhistle's first-floor shop. Here, Helvetia Appleyard, daughter of a printer and a Girton graduate, decides to educate the promising grocery clerk. In love, they find the parents opposed to their marriage. Taking their problem to kind Peter Hope, they all consult. Tommy's bright ideas bring reconciliation all around in addition to a new printer for *Good Humour.*

Miss Ramsbotham's story is the tale of the capable, likable woman reporter who is too reasonable to be swept off her feet by infatuation. But the improbable happens; she falls in love with the impossible Reginald Peters, younger, conceited, rude. The staff tolerates him only because Miss Ramsbotham blossoms into loveliness because of him. When Reggie falls in love with a shop girl, he leaves at Miss Ramsbotham's suggestion for Canada to allow him time to decide between the two women. Miss Ramsbotham, having decided to surrender him to the younger woman, sensibly throws herself into writing "Letters to Clorinda," a woman's column for the paper. Dressing stylishly for the advertisers, she grows younger and more beautiful; but Miss Peggy of the bun shop fattens on chocolate and cream. Reggie, returned from Canada now finds Peggy repulsive; Miss Ramsbotham, beautiful—and so do other men. Wiser, contented, she rejects Reggie—and other men—and remains with her newspaper job.

When Joey Loveredge, perennial bachelor, returns from a vacation married, he no longer frequents the Autolycus Club, and he ignores his old friends. The staff finally worms from him that his bride thinks newspaper friends not quite respectable. The group then assumes aristocratic names and makes itself acceptable at the Loveredge dinner parties— until Mrs. Loveredge's secret social find comes to dinner, a genuine member of the aristocracy, who is related to half the names the staff has assumed. The Lady Mary, however, is good-natured; and after a private conference with Tommy, she plays along until a successful ending is worked out.

"The Babe," annoyed that Miss Hope allows him to hang about the editorial offices but never asks him to contribute, learns that the staff very much wants the advertising account of Mr. Jowett. When the staff despairs of getting it, Miss Ramsbotham points out that a young woman might not be thrown out of Jowett's office. "The Babe," with his youthful face, decides to make up as a girl to get the coveted account. The disguise works; and pleased with his success, "The Babe" decides to fool the boys at the Autolycus Club, who, suspecting the truth, pretend to be deceived. Complications follow on both sides, and each has its share of funny and embarrassing incidents.

When Dick Danvers, seedily dressed but with the distinct marks of a gentleman, submits a story to Tommy, the two fall in love. His continued contributions and his presence in the office win him friends, Tommy's love and Peter Hope's fears of losing his Tommy. After Dick Danvers has proposed and been accepted, "the woman of his past" appears. In a dramatic scene Tommy and Dick give each other up for the sake of the other woman's reputation and their coming child. After fifteen years, in which Tommy remains faithful to the memory, Dick reappears with his daughter and is welcomed by Tommy, the staff, and the aging Peter Hope, who envisions his paper carried on by his devoted daughter Tommy and her husband.

At the end of the novel, a break in the narrative point of view occurs. The story has been told in third person:

Were this an artistic story, here, of course, one would write "Finis." But in the workaday world one never knows the ending till it comes. Had it been otherwise, I doubt if I could have found courage to tell you this story of Tommy. It is not all true—at least, I do not suppose so. One drifts unconsciously a little way into dreamland when one sits down to recall the happenings of long ago; while Fancy, with a sly wink, whispers ever and again to Memory: "Let me tell this incident—picture that scene: I can make it so much more interesting than you would." But Tommy—how can I put it without saying too much: there is someone I think of when I speak of her? To remember only her dear wounds, and not the healing of them, would have been a task too painful. I love to dwell on their next meeting. Flipp, passing him on the steps, did not know him,

the tall, sunburnt gentleman with the sweet, grave-faced little
girl.[5]

Though this paragraph marks the only time the author in the
first person intrudes, the reader is not completely surprised.
A few comments prepare for this switch in narrative method,
such as the one at the finish of Tommy's scoop in inter-
viewing the prince:". . . she arrived about midnight, suffering from a sense of self-importance, traces of which to this
day are still discernible" (44–45)—or the reference to the
present in Miss Ramsbotham's story, which concludes, "She
is still Miss Ramsbotham. Bald-headed gentlemen feel
young again talking to her: she is so sympathetic, so big-
minded, so understanding. Then, hearing the clock strike,
tear themselves from her with a sigh, and return—some of
them—to stupid shrewish wives" (158–59). Such comments
extend the personalities into a living present and seem to
make the omniscient third-person narrator a participator
in the group.

Quite possibly, as in the scenes from Bohemian London
in *Paul Kelver*, the characters from *Tommy and Co.* could be
identified with various writers with whom Jerome worked
on *The Idler* and *To-day*. Part memory, part fancy, as the
author says, is probably the truth of the matter. Autobiographical or not, *Tommy and Co.* ranks very early, if it is
not a first, in the type of novel since become popular in
which the newspaper world provides a fascinating milieu.[6]

Peter Hope and Tommy present again a combination of
father and child. The father is a dreamer; he is revered
and respected but needs practical friends—his clever,
shrewd daughter, in this case—to help him make his way in
the world. For example, Peter is shocked at Miss Ramsbotham's compromising suggestion of a woman's page, and
her pragmatic "Make your paper a success first. You can
make it a power afterwards" (146) elicits this response:

Poor Peter groaned—old Peter, the dreamer of dreams. But
for the thought of Tommy! one day to be left alone . . . Peter
most assuredly would have risen in his wrath, would have said

to his distinguished-looking temptress, "Get thee behind me, Miss Ramsbotham. My journalistic instinct whispers to me that your scheme, judged by the mammon of unrighteousness, is good. It is a new departure. Ten years hence half the London journals will have adopted it. There is money in it. But what of that? Shall I for mere dross sell my editorial soul, turn the temple of the Mighty Pen into a den of—of milliners! Good morning, Miss Ramsbotham. I grieve for you. I grieve for you as for a fellow-worker once inspired by devotion to a noble calling, who has fallen from her high estate. Good morning, madam."

So Peter thought as he sat tattooing with his finger-tips upon the desk; but only said—"It would have to be well done." (147)

Tommy appeals with her cockney expressions, her sense of humor, her sensitivity. But she is not mawkishly drawn; even in the final story she escapes a melodramatic treatment, partly by her common sense, partly by the comedy of the piano lessons which the staff has decided she needs in order to be more refined and at which she performs so badly but so doggedly.

The Jewish family story, which forms a minor inset, probably owes something to Jerome's friendship with Israel Zangwill and his brother, for Zangwill had written stories of the London ghetto lives of the Jews in the 1890's. Jerome's story is sympathetic, humorously told. The old folks are not stereotypes, but they exhibit a bit of local color in their surroundings and their talk. The best of the minor character studies is probably that of Miss Ramsbotham, who is deftly drawn. She is developed mostly by the comments others make of her and by their reaction to her situation. Miss Ramsbotham's letter when she first falls in love, her conversation when others try to reason with her, and her behavior are very real. She appears, perhaps, the most lifelike of any character in the book. The members of the Autolycus Club are sketched in with just enough detail so that their personalities can be distinguished. Their banter is amusing—no cleverer than it should be to sound genuine. It is Jeromian humor, as well-known in its time as the longer-remembered Shavian wit. Indeed, *Tommy and Co.* is good entertainment.

III   They and I (1909)

They and I is even less a novel than *Tommy and Co.* However, if the form of a novel may provide a vehicle for propaganda or thesis, there seems no reason why it may not also
be the means for humorous reflections on sundry light topics.
The topics rise naturally from the situations and conversation, and the novel deals with lifelike characters at the
normal low pitch of life rather than at some peak of tension.
The title and the ideas seem surprisingly modern, for the
novel is a family novel with the theme of the generation gap.
The father of the family—an author, a teller of humorous
tales, and approximately the age of Jerome K. Jerome—
narrates the story in first person. The action commences
with the decision to buy a new house, something in the
country for the family. The family consists of the narrator;
the Little Mother; Dick, twenty and down from the university after a disappointing year; Robina, eighteen; and
Veronica, nine. The house decided upon—after much discussion over Dick's concern for a billiard room, Robina's
for a ballroom, and Veronica's modest request for a room of
her own—is in Berkshire; it needs remodeling but has a
cottage that can be used while the big house is redone.

Summer vacation is launched with the Little Mother left
in the city, for life in the run-down cottage is thought to be
too robust for her. In the country, Robina does the cooking,
Dick learns farming from a neighbor, and Veronica tries to
be as helpful as possible. The father sends an architect
to plan the remodeling of the main house; he is young,
and he is attractive to all but Robina. But the architect finds
it necessary to spend considerable time with the family in
order to redesign the house.

The family reacts as do most city dwellers to the country.
The cow wakes them too early; the owls hoot all night.
Robina finds that milking requires skill, and all yield to
'Enery 'Opkins, the only one who can manage the obstinate
donkey. 'Enery is a disappointment to them only in the fact
that his accent is cockney, from "Camden Tahn," not Berkshire, though he obligingly offers to read a book in order to
learn Berkshire dialect. Jerome's cheeky gamin, consistently

well drawn in his works, this time faces competition for appeal from nine-year-old Veronica. Her particular action that results in the most inconvenience stems from her having overheard a farm woman's advice to Robina about using a bit of gunpowder to clear a stopped chimney. After Veronica has conned a small boy into getting the powder, they place it under a stove lid. Thanks to the brown paper wrapping about it, they escape injury, though not without damage to the boy's velvet suit and the near destruction of the kitchen.

The mixed emotions resulting are familiar to every reader—gratitude, annoyance, anger. Veronica receives a lecture about the rewards of doing right, about retribution, and about Providence. She concludes this world is a puzzling one. When her father suggests that she turn her efforts to writing a book, the idea appeals to her. She decides to call the book "Why the Man in the Moon Looks Sat Upon." In a letter to her father Veronica writes: "I have written a lot of the book. It promises to be very interesting. It is all a dream. He is just an ordinary grown-up father. Neither better nor worse. And he goes up and up. It is a pleasant sensation. Till he reaches the moon. And there everything is different. It is the children that know everything. And are always right. And the grown-ups have to do all what they tell them. They are kind but firm. It is very good for him. I put down everything that occurs to me. Like you suggested. There is quite a lot of it. . . ."[7]

Dick's interest in the neighbor's farm includes the farmer's daughter, Janie. Robina, in the meantime, has gotten over her annoyance with the young architect—in fact, she is in love with Bute. With two of his children in love, the father finds them seeking him out as confidant. He talks to them of the idealism of lovers, of passion, of renunciation. Robina concludes about love:

"Then all love is needless. We could do better without it, choose with more discretion. If it is only something that worries us for a little while and then passes, what is the sense of it"?

"You could ask the same question of Life itself," I said; "something that worries us for a little while, then passes. Perhaps the

worry, as you call it, has its uses. Volcanic upheavals are necessary
to the making of a world. . . . That explosion of Youth's pent-up
forces that we term Love serves to the making of man and woman.
It does not die, it takes new shape." (212)

After talking with Dick about marriage, the father reflects
on the generation that lives in an affluence not known to
their parents as young people:

I feel so sorry for Dick—for the tens of thousands of happy,
healthy cared-for lads of whom Dick is the type. There must be
millions of youngsters in the world who have never known hunger,
except as an appetiser to dinner; who have never felt what it was
to be tired, without the knowledge that a comfortable bed was
awaiting them. . . . Terrible things occur out there to little men
and little women who have no pretty nursery to live in. People
push and shove you about, will even tread on your toes if you are
not careful. . . . One has to fend for oneself, out there; earn one's
dinner before one eats it, never quite sure of the week after next.
Terrible things take place, out there. (250 and 252)

When the big house is finished, each member of the family
concludes that the terrace will be his favorite spot. Veronica,
reflecting that Dick and Robina may soon be leaving, provides the conclusion to the book: "'I suppose,' said Veronica,
'that if anything was to happen to Robina, everything would
fall on me.' 'It would be a change, Veronica,' I suggested.
'Hitherto it is you who have done most of the falling.' 'Suppose I've got to see about growing up,' said Veronica" (255).
    The novel provides light entertainment, but the humor is
less boisterous than in some of Jerome's work. The topics
are, however, perennially amusing. The individual traits of
character are made distinct; Veronica, in this brief
novel, stands out as quite a remarkable portrait of a girl at
the awkward age of nine. Were the author and date not
known, *They and I* might very well sell for current, popular
reading.

IV   All Roads Lead to Calvary *(1919)*

Jerome K. Jerome wrote his next novel at the end of World
War I after having served with the French ambulance corps.

In *All Roads Lead to Calvary*, Jerome's protagonist, a young
woman journalist, faces crises arising from political issues
and decisions she must make for herself in regard to the new
freedom for women and the loosening of old religious ties.
Of all Jerome's novels, this one comes closest to being a
polemical novel.[8] The protagonist ponders most of the questions that Paul Kelver does about religion and love. She does
not herself experience poverty but feels strongly her ob-
ligation to help the poor. She lacks the sense of humor that
Paul Kelver has, and her journalistic circle is more intellectual than that of Tommy and Peter Hope. Indeed, all her
roads lead to Calvary. "I felt sad when I wrote it," Jerome
explained to an admirer of the novel.[9] Nevertheless, the book
presents a convincing heroine coping with topical questions.

Joan Allway, a young journalist, wandering in Chelsea of a
Sunday evening, stops at an old church in Cheyne Walk,
having decided to write a feature article on old churches
of London. Joan listens sympathetically to Mary Stopperton,
the little old pew-opener who has known the Thomas
Carlyles and the Leigh Hunts. Although Joan stays for the
evening service, she believes Christianity is dead; but she
admits the need of the soul for some idealism. She laughs
as the minister reads the story of Jonah. One sentence,
though, from his sermon, "All roads lead to Calvary," strikes
her; and as she leaves the church, she has an uncanny feeling
in the evening light that she has somewhere before known
the old minister—perhaps in her childhood. The thought
causes her to remember her childhood reactions against a
strict Nonconformist theology. She recalls shocking her
nurse by playing at tempting the devil while quite aware of
her mischievousness. She especially remembers an experience like that of Tannhauser's in which satanic sounds of
musical discord struggle with the "faint but conquering
Pilgrim's onward march."[10]

A Cambridge graduate, she has come to London encouraged by other woman in journalism: Flossie Lessing, Madge
Singleton, and Mrs. Denton, the dean of journalists. They
talk seriously of the high aims of journalism and feel they
are thoroughly modern. At a luncheon she meets Miss Greyson, who assists her brother, Francis, with his paper. He,

too, is an idealist, with "the face of a dreamer, but about the mouth there was suggestion of the fighter" (49). He accepts her "Chelsea Churches" and puts her to writing his column, "Letters to Clorinda"; but he realistically sends her to Carleton, editor of the powerful chain of newspapers. She talks with Carleton, who listens to her desire to talk to the people: "'All right,' he said. 'Go ahead. You shall have your tub, and a weekly audience of a million readers for as long as you can keep them interested. Up with everything you like, and down with everything you don't. Be careful not to land me in a libel suit. Call the whole Bench of Bishops hypocrites, and all the ground landlords thieves, if you will: but don't mention names. . . . One stipulation,' he went on, 'that every article is headed with your photograph'" (54–55).

Joan protests the sort of publicity that cheapens by the use of her looks. He reminds her that Joan of Arc, her namesake of France, "put on a becoming suit of armour and got upon a horse where everyone could see her. Chivalry isn't dead. You modern women are ashamed of yourselves— ashamed of your sex. You don't give it a chance. Revive it. Stir the young men's blood. Their souls will follow" (56). Consenting to let her picture aid her column, she leaves the office, full of ideas of how to change the sordid city that she observes around her.

She begins, full of pity, to plan her work. "This monstrous conspiracy, once of the Sword, of the Church, now of the Press, that put all Government into the hands of a few stuffy old gentlemen, politicians, leaders, writers, without sympathy or understanding: it was time that it was swept away. She would raise a new standard. It should be, not 'Listen to me, oh ye dumb,' but 'Speak to me. Tell me your hidden hopes, your fears, your dreams. Tell me your experience, your thoughts born of knowledge, of suffering'" (60). She is disillusioned as she walks about the city seeing, through swinging doors, foul interiors, crowded with men and women taking their evening pleasure; noticing the colored posters outside theaters with their vulgarity and lewdness; the competitive advertising signs; and the newsboy, selling the papers like hot cakes because the headlines promise the details of a "Orrible murder of a woman. Shockin' details" (71).

The next lesson Joan learns of the world involves her more personally, though the problem begins with her professional introduction to the rising young Labour party member, Robert Phillips, from the mines of Wales. Robert Phillips, slated to be a new cabinet member, may be severely handicapped by his crude wife, a former barmaid. Joan and Robert inspire each other, as Mrs. Phillips and their daughter see. Mrs. Phillips likes Joan because Joan can help her husband; and Joan honestly tries to improve Mrs. Phillips, fails at the job, but recognizes that pity keeps her from abusing the trust Mrs. Phillips has in her. In Paris, Joan meets Phillips and almost consents to becoming his mistress. When her old friends warn her of appearances, she becomes offended, aloof. She takes a trip with her father, and she begins to know him much better than she had and hears the story of her parents' love.

Mrs. Phillips, ill, sends for Joan, asking her to see Robert Phillips on to success if she should die. On a second visit to the sick woman, Joan discovers that Mrs. Phillips is poisoning herself from the make-up box. Joan suspects the daughter, Hilda, who idolizes Joan, of planting in her mother's head the idea of sacrificing herself for her husband's sake. Joan has a bitter self-confrontation, what she calls her Garden of Gethsemane, and determines to give up Robert Phillips. She confronts Mrs. Phillips, makes her desist in her self-destruction, and sends for Robert. Robert and Joan renounce their love for each other.

Joan throws herself into the movement for woman suffrage. She tries to love her cousin Arthur, who is very much in love with her. She succeds in encouraging him to help her father and to join the family firm in place of her.

Joan becomes more cynical as Carleton's chain of newspapers engulfs even Greyson's idealistic journal. At one of Mrs. Denton's intellectual Fridays, she meets Hilda Phillips, the daughter who once idolized her and despised her own mother. More cynical than Joan, Hilda confronts Joan with the question as to why, if she loved Robert Phillips, she had not allowed the sacrifice of her mother to continue.

Forced to answer, Joan speaks of love's intentions and love's failure to live up to them, of the accidents that occur that turn lives into ironic situations:

"It's the very absurdity of it all that makes the mystery of life— that renders it so hopeless for us to attempt to find our way through it by our own judgment. It is like the ants making all their clever, laborious plans, knowing nothing of chickens and the gardener's spade. That is why we have to cling to the life we can order for ourselves—the life within us. Truth, Justice, Pity. They are the strong things, the eternal things, the things we've got to sacrifice ourselves for—serve with our bodies and our souls.

"Don't think me a prig . . . I'm talking as if I knew all about it. I don't really. I grope in the dark; and now and then . . . I catch a glint of light. We are powerless in ourselves. It is only God working through us that enables us to be of any use. All we can do is to keep ourselves kind and clean and free from self, waiting for Him to come to us." . . .

"Tell me," [Hilda] said. "What is God?"

"A Labourer, together with man, according to Saint Paul," Joan answered. (277-78)

About London, the talk of war begins. Joan blames news-papers for their sensationalism. Friendships break up as war is declared: Francis Greyson joins the air corps, Arthur All-way the merchant marines, and Phillips becomes a captain. Arthur returns, becomes a conscientious objector, and is killed by an angry mob. Joan, who joins the nursing corps, serves in a hospital on the front in the Argonne. She talks with patients, and they, all eager to see the war over, blame patriotism, the newspapers. One old fellow speaks up, though, and says, "I'll tell you who makes all the wars, it's you and me, my dears: we make the wars. We love them. That's why we open our mouths and swallow all the twaddle that the papers give us; and cheer the fine, black-coated gentlemen when they tell us it's our sacred duty to kill Ger-mans, or Italians, or Russians, or anybody else. We are just crazy to kill something. . . . No, my dears, it's we make the wars. You and me, my dears" (329).

In the midst of the worst fighting, Joan and some of the wounded in a shelter have a vision of a peasant who speaks to them: "The light from the oil lamp, suspended from the ceiling fell upon his face. He wore a peasant's blouse. It seemed to her a face she knew. . . . It was his eyes that for long years afterwards still haunted her. She did not notice at the time what language he was speaking. But there were none who did not understand him" (333-34). The peasant talks to them of their trying to explain the world in which so much suffering exists, and of how some blame God for allowing evil, making his creatures weak and sinful:

"There is no God, apart from Man.
"God is a spirit. His dwelling-place is in man's heart. We are His fellow-labourers. It is through man that He shall one day rule the world. . . .
"God whispers to you 'Be pitiful. Be merciful. Be just.' But you answer Him: 'If I am pitiful, I lose my time and money. If I am merciful, I forego advantage to myself. If I am just, I lessen my own profit, and another passes me in the race.'
"And yet in your inmost thoughts you know that you are wrong; that love of self brings you no peace. . . . God pleads to you. He is waiting for your help" (334–35).

There is shouting and laughter outside, and the war is over. They look around, and the peasant has gone. No man saw him leave.

Several of Joan's friends have died in the war. She lives now with her father. Both are glad to leave London and return to the family home in Liverpool. Joan tells her father of her engagement to Francis Greyson, who joins them as they are planning to make part of the family business into a company to be shared by workers and management alike, and the new ways stem from the Allway Scheme, based on Christian love.

The action of *All Roads Lead to Calvary* centers on Joan Allway; in fact, all activity is seen through the consciousness of Joan. Not the chapter headings but the title gives structure to the novel. The fact that the time element is shorter than in the novels *Paul Kelver* and *Anthony John*, which begin in childhood, concentrates the experiences on the protagonist's initiation into maturity. The unifying

experience which begins and ends the novel is the protagonist's recognition of a truth spoken to the soul. In the first
instance, the minister leaves Joan with the words she cannot
forget (the title of the book) and with the feeling of having
known the speaker some time in her past. The last instance
provides another message, this time from the peasant whose
face seems vaguely familiar; and he formulates a definition
of God that gives direction to her thinking.

In the middle of the novel's action, Joan has remembered
to ask her father if he had ever known the minister who had
said those words. As the train pulls out and he has not replied, she notices her father standing motionless, as if he
also is struck by a strange memory. Readers of Jerome's
The Passing of the Third Floor Back, or the thousands who
have seen the play, will recall that "The Stranger" of the
play leaves the impression on all whom he meets that they
have known him before—in their more innocent days; and
he, too, recalls them to their better selves. In *All Roads
Lead to Calvary*, these moments of inspiration give the
novel its framework. The opening experience plants the
thought which takes on personal meaning in Joan's Garden
of Gethsemane experience. The final experience seems to
give direction to her life.

The thesis of the novel emerges from the action: the necessity for mankind to renounce self for the sake of truth,
justice, mercy; for God himself needs man's choice of his
better instincts in an imperfect world in which God is powerless for good without man's help. Jerome has, in earlier
works, stressed the need of man to choose good rather than
evil, but in this novel he defines God as a limited, imperfect Being. Joan Allway, through whose experiences the
theme is presented, is a convincing character, though not so
appealing as Paul Kelver. She is self-confident, almost smug.
Still, Jerome seems to capture the enthusiasm and assurance
of young intellectuals, Joan and her friends, who are in a
position to effect changes in government—to influence a
newspaper public. Joan's rationalization of her step-by-
step progress toward becoming Robert Phillips' mistress
and her analyses of her own motives, her good intentions,
are realistic.

In the action, the return to Mary Stopperton, the little pew-opener who appears at the beginning of the novel, as a touchstone to truth or humility, seems a bit melodramatic, even contrived. For example, it is a lonely Christmas day and Joan, alone in the city, decides to visit her old friend Mary. A collection of the poor has gathered with Mary for Sunday supper, and they argue about religion. The group, though, has become pointedly allegorical. The old fanatic, Mr. Baptiste, speaks: "'A strange supper-party,' he said. 'Cyril the Apostate; and Julius who strove against the High Priest and the Pharisees; and Inez a dancer before the people; and Joanna a daughter of the rulers, gathered together in the house of one Mary a servant of the lord. Are you, too, a Christian?' he asked of Joan. 'Not yet,' answered Joan. 'But I hope to be, one day.' She spoke without thinking, not quite knowing what she meant. But it came back to her in after years" (171–72).

As for the minor characters, the group of young women journalists speak winningly, and in a fashion that has not become dated. Flossie's love for Sam resembles Miss Ramsbotham's story in *Tommy and Co.* Francis Greyson remains too lightly sketched, not so believable as her cousin Arthur Allway, who has a less important part. Arthur Allway and Joan's father remind us of Ralph Touchett and his father in Henry James' *Portrait of a Lady* (1881). Robert Phillips, as the self-made man who is determined not to become corrupt, has some similarity to Dr. Hal of *Paul Kelver* but lacks the warmth of that character.

Phillips acquires dignity with his decision to remain with his disgraceful Nan, but the reader's interest in him consequently lessens. In what seems by 1919 a familiar statement by Jerome, Phillips analyzes his love of the two women: "It isn't good that man should worship a woman. He can't serve God and woman. Their interests are liable to clash. Nan's my helpmate—just a loving woman that the Lord brought to me and gave me when I was alone—that I still love. I didn't know it till last night. She will never stand in my way. I haven't to put her against my duty. She will leave me free to obey the voice that calls to me. And no man can hear that voice but himself" (256-57). To Joan, "It was

this man alone to whom she had ever felt drawn—this man
of the people, with that suggestion about him of something
primitive, untamed, causing her always in his presence that
faint, compelling thrill of fear, who stirred her blood as none
of the polished men of her own class had ever done. His
kind, strong, ugly face: it moved beside her: its fearless,
tender eyes now pleading, now commanding" (246).

The novel holds interest until Joan makes her sacrifice,
her private Gethsemane; but after this crisis, when she
seems at loose ends, the novel lacks focus. The war brings together threads of the novel—people are disposed of as they
survive or are destroyed in the war, but the effect is rather
of clutter than otherwise. The war experiences of Joan as a
nurse in the Argonne are realistic; but they are brief, summary, and come too late in the action of the novel to revive
interest.

All Roads Lead to Calvary remains readable, but it is a
thesis novel; and, more than any of the Jerome novels, it
seems a period piece.[11]

V Anthony John *(1923)*

Anthony John, another polemical novel, returns to the
setting in the industrial North of England where Jerome was
born and where his father had failed economically in the
mines. Depression followed World War I, and Jerome concentrates in this novel upon the responsibility of the wealthy
and capable in a society in which poverty prevails. The
protagonist is again an alter ego for the author, but this
time—unlike Paul Kelver who recalls Jerome's London
childhood—the boy, who is a dreamer, early recognizes that
he must put aside dreams in order to rise from poverty. He
deliberately cultivates the best ways of getting on. The book
seems almost the projection of a Paul Kelver (or a Jerome)
if Paul Kelver and his family had remained in the North.

Anthony John is the Christian name of the baby Strong'
nth'arm, born fighting. "He's come to stop," says the nurse,
who has observed babies in this family and in many other
families of the poor born too weak to struggle. Anthony John,
the only child, begins his childhood years watching his father work in his blacksmith shop. The father stems from an-

cient yeoman stock, even gentry in times past; for a local legend relates that Monk Anthony Strong'nth'arm, who resisted the invasion of Percival de Combler, was the ancestor of the Coombers who now own the great hall where Anthony John's mother had been in service before her marriage.

Anthony's mother, when times are particularly hard, visits Sir William Coomber and comes back with food and clothes. Young Anthony confuses Sir William with God, from whom all blessings flow. In fact, the boy asks many embarrassing questions of his elders about God. The Strong'nth'arms are Nonconformists; but the mother, in order to advance themselves for the sake of the boy, joins the Church of England. The father raises no objections since being a chapel-goer seems not to have prospered him. When Mr. Strong'nth'arm falls sick, the King of the Gnomes comes to help in the shop and about the house. Both Anthony and his mother see him many times. Mrs. Plumbery, the midwife, knows of him, too. In fact, the poor are often aided by him when in distress. He is labeled "Wandering Peter," and sometimes in reports is confused with Christ.

Business becomes better in the shop after the father recovers, but Mrs. Strong'nth'arm suffers humiliation when she tries to enter Anthony in Miss Warmington's private school. Miss Warmington deeply regrets, but other parents would object to a son of a blacksmith and a former servant. Miss Warmington relents upon facing the bright little boy; but when she asks if he would like to go to school there, Anthony stubbornly replies, "No, thank you." The vicar suggests young Tetteridge for a tutor, a dreamy boy not much older than Anthony. They get along splendidly and become friends. Anthony's father dies of an accident in the shop, and young Tetteridge manages to find scholarships to a grammar school for both of them.

Anthony does well at school and makes friends, after a schoolboy fight defending his mother, now turned milliner and occasional charwoman. The wealthy solicitor's son Edward Mowbray and his sister Betty like him, and they all talk a great deal about helping the poor. Edward, more radical, thinks politics will answer the needs of the poor; Betty believes the rich must provide decent housing and better wages; and Anthony, who favors Betty's view, decides to fight his idealistic instinct in order to become one of the prosperous who can help. He soon demonstrates that he has the Midas touch.

Anthony John establishes Tetteridge in a school for the rising poor, such as they both had been, in a large house in which his mother becomes housekeeper for them all. Tetteridge marries an ambitious young wife, and soon their school becomes too refined for the poor. Anthony, who goes into Mr. Mowbray's law office, works his way into a junior partnership, taking the place intended for his friend Edward Mowbray, who has died during his college career. Anthony becomes a town favorite, promoting schemes for better housing, civic improvement, even making the town an inland port and redirecting a main artery of the railway through their city.

The Sir William Coomber family returns from European travels, but not before Anthony, agent for the estate, has had a vision in the garden of young Eleanor, the lovely daughter. Betty Mowbray and Anthony have assumed their deep friendship would end in marriage, and Anthony's mother and Betty's father both favor it. But Anthony really finds romantic love with Eleanor Coomber. Betty recognizes that Anthony is not in love with her but has thought she would be a helpmeet; and they remain good friends. Anthony marries Eleanor, and they prosper with Anthony doing much good, as he had planned. They have three children, the oldest a dreamer, who in turn encounters Wandering Peter, or Christ. This son, who dies at the age of eight, is the child to whom Anthony has become most attached. When Eleanor becomes ill, Anthony bargains with God to finish certain projects for the poor in exchange for her recovery. Eleanor recovers, but Anthony's architect, who has talked with Anthony about Christianity, has been killed on the job. He has, however, left Anthony a legacy of his beliefs about the imperfect God who needs man's aid to help Him make a more perfect world.

Anthony observes that his efforts to help society by modern housing projects have failed in that the housing projects have become in time new slums. What the poor need are not more amenities but education, the aid of knowing friends. He decides to give up his wealthy clientele, his membership on boards, if necessary his wife and children, to serve the poor by living near them—by becoming a solicitor for the poor. Eleanor, and the two spoiled children, must also make sacrifices. The children, grown up, can go their way. Eleanor, too, decides to sacrifice: "And suddenly it came to her that this was the Great Adventure of the World, calling to the brave and hopeful to follow, heedless, where God's trumpet led. Somewhere—perhaps near, perhaps far—there lay the Promised Land. It might be theirs to find it—at least to see it from afar. If not—! Their feet should help to mark the road. Yes, she too would give up her possessions; put fear behind her. Together, hand in hand, they would go forward, joyously."[12]

Anthony John is told from the point of view of an omniscient author; but Anthony, man and boy, is the center of all the action. As in *All Roads Lead to Calvary*, no chapter headings form the framework as they do in Jerome's first three novels. The family name, Strong'nth'arm, however, suggests a unifying core. It is significant that the crest of the old Danish family of Clapa, the ancestors of Jerome, shows an upraised arm grasping a battle ax. We might surmise, too, that Jerome had in mind the comparison of Hamlet the dreamer and the success of Fortinbras, strong in arm, the man of action. At any rate, the compelling drive in all the action is the protagonist's determination to submerge the dreamer. That Anthony John can exploit his charm, capitalize on his strength, and remain a likable figure, depends in part on Jerome's careful portrayal in the first part of the book of the situation of the struggling poor: of the people like Anthony John's father who work hard, have ideas, but lack the power to promote their inventions; of the shadowy lines of respectability that make for class differences; of the half humorous, half wistful way Jerome has of describing young boys. In *Paul Kelver* the family had fallen from a respectable position but had maintained by considerable sacrifice the appearances of gentry. In *Anthony John*, the Strong'nth'arm family can no longer pretend to social distinction. Their struggle is that of the rising classes—one of the poor moving into middle-class

respectability. The humiliations suffered until young
Anthony fights his way into a position of respect are strik-
ingly depicted.

Mrs. Strong'nth'arm stands out as one of Jerome's most
memorable characters. She cannot forget her servant training, yet is angry at her own subservience, which she means
to curb. She bows to Miss Warmington when she means to
meet her as an equal. In old age, when her son marries into
the Coomber family at the great hall where she was formerly
a servant, she cannot be persuaded to stay overnight nor
even to use the front door. The father dislikes being remind-
ed of the former gentility of his family, and is bitter, sometimes complaining. Like Paul Kelver's father, he is one of
the unlucky ones, but he lacks Mr. Kelver's optimism, his
jauntiness. The pious aunt, with her atheist husband who
live in a converted railway car provide interest and are convincingly real. Anthony John, himself, appeals with his
silent ways, his rather comical sturdiness, his determination.

The first part of the book, up to Anthony John's success in
the law office and his friendship with the Mowbrays, even
through his romantic courtship of Eleanor Coomber, is well
structured. At this point, however, the novel moves into its
cause. The novel now presents not only the necessity of
the rich to work for the poor, and not only the thesis of the
limited God who needs man's help, a similar position to
that of the previous novel, *All Roads Lead to Calvary*, but
the plan of capitalism to improve the living conditions of
the poor is shown to be futile. Jerome appeals to the type of
Christianity sponsored by Tolstoy; in fact, Jerome states his
indebtedness through the character Mr. Landripp, his architect:

Two thousand years after Christ's death one man . . . the Russian
writer Tolstoy, had made serious attempts to live the life com-
manded by Christ. And all Christendom stood staring at him in
stupefied amazement. If Christ had been God's scheme for the
reformation of a race that He Himself had created prone to evil
then it had tragically failed. . . . There is a story by Jean Paul
Richter. . . . The man in the story . . . meets Christ. And the
Christ is still sad and troubled. The man asks why, and Christ
confesses to him. He has been looking for God and cannot find

Him. And the man comforts Him. Together they will seek God, and yet will find Him . . . Christ's God. . . . He is the God—the genius, if you prefer the word, of the human race. He is seeking— still seeking to make man in His own image. . . . The moral law within us, the voice of pity, of justice is His only means of helping us. The God I am seeking asks, not gives. (208–211 *passim.*)

In a pattern of reversal, the action of Anthony John follows. What Anthony has gained by the strength of his arm and considered blessings, he now gives up. They had been gifts that he could give to the poor. It was the same with his love for Eleanor. Rather than making her the sharer of his visions, he had wanted to come to her with gifts, so that she might be grateful to him. "God wanted him. . . . He would get rid of all his affairs—of everything literally. Not for the sake of the poor. . . . From time immemorial the rich had flung money to the poor, and the poor had ever increased in number, had sunk even poorer . . . . Love, service, were the only living gifts. It was for his own sake . . that he must flee from his great possessions" (255–56). In this decision, the assumption is that Anthony John has won his greatest victory.

Though this novel most thoroughly reveals Jerome's religious thinking, and though by the end of the book, the main character has become the mouthpiece for Jerome, the first part of the novel recaptures much of the charm of *Paul Kelver*—it has the light touch that is the hallmark of Jerome's successful writing. Jerome is nearly always successful with scenes of the working class, and these characters are from the North country that his parents knew and that he visited. Schoolboy scenes, too, evoke the intensity of feeling of the lad who is the underdog—in this case a "cropped" or charity-foundation scholar. The scenes with Edward and Betty Mowbray match some of the better scenes of the young intellectuals of *All Roads Lead to Calvary* who are serious but not pompous. The characters of the great hall, the Coomber family, are less convincingly presented. Anthony's feelings and his mother's antagonism seem realistic, but Eleanor's brother of the Horse Guards seems brought in for a stereotyped speech on love and the class system. The mother, an American woman haunted by an old fear of having Negro

blood, seems unsuccessful. She probably stems from
Jerome's reaction to the situation in the American South
which he had observed on his lecture tour. It comes as a
surprise to the reader of other of Jerome's novels and plays
to find that Anthony John chooses as his wife the idolized
woman, Eleanor Coomber, rather than the companionable
helpmeet.

The next generation introduced, Anthony's and Eleanor's
children, are simply crowded in, primarily, we feel, to allow
the King of the Gnomes or Wandering Peter to reappear to
the dreamy son of Anthony—a boy too ethereal for this world.
Indeed, *Anthony John*, as well as *All Roads Lead to Calvary*,
fails to develop interest in the numerous characters introduced late in the book, or in the attempt to bring to a
conclusion all the lives of minor individuals whose lives
have at some time crossed paths with the lives of the main
characters. Perhaps Jerome's experience of writing the well-
made play with its small number of characters who can easily
be brought to a balance at the end of the play hampers him
when he tries for the neat ending in the larger span of the
novel. The three-generation span introduces more characters
and more situations than Jerome can master artistically.

Jerome recollects in *My Life and Times* that he had always
dreamed of being an editor. "My mother gave me a desk
on my sixth birthday, and I started a newspaper in partnership with a little old maiden aunt of mine. . . . My mother
liked our first number. 'I am sure he was meant to be a
preacher,' she said to my father. 'It comes to the same thing,'
said my father. 'The newspaper is going to be the new pulpit'" (194–95). Jerome did become a successful editor; but
the novel became his pulpit.

CHAPTER 6

The Idler in Retrospect

I The Complete Jerome

IN concluding a study of Jerome K. Jerome, three aspects
should be considered; the complete Jerome; his place in
his time; and his position today. Humorist, editor, playwright, novelist, lecturer, and emissary for war and peace—
the scope of Jerome's work seems broad; but fragmented it
is not. From the humor of young men boating to the ser-
monizing of a mysterious stranger, Jerome's characters comprise a picture in which there is no discrepancy between the
laughter on the one hand and the moralizing on the other.
The binding thread is Jerome's attitude. "Pity is akin to
love" is a phrase that recurs in Jerome. Its obvious applica-
tion occurs in incident after incident in Jerome's fiction
and plays, but the laughter, too, becomes a part of it, not
only for what his humor is but for what it is not. The jesting
never mocks, for Jerome is not bitter. When he tells of cats
or dogs, errand boys, or boating young men, the laughter is
good-natured, tempered with tolerance. Like Rosaline's
Berowne, he is a merry man "within the limits of becoming
mirth."

In some of Jerome's works he is all humor, as in *Three Men
in a Boat* and *Stage-Land;* in some he is all serious, as in
All Roads Lead to Calvary; but he is best, perhaps, where
the mixture prevails, as in *Paul Kelver, On the Stage—And
Off, Tommy and Co.,* or most of *The Idler* collections. Perhaps the charm of these works comes from the overlay of
nostalgia which can be tender about yesterday's mistakes
and smile.

On reform, Jerome is also both serious and humorous. The
battle of the sexes he can treat as standard comic material,
but he is never brutal. His major reform efforts in the plays

and in one or two novels concern the position of woman, and he works for the dignity of her life. Like George Meredith in his *Essay on Comedy*, Jerome believes that "where women are on the road to an equal footing with man in attainments and in liberty pure Comedy flourishes"; but he is exasperated at the ignorance of Victorian women and the protective shell around them. He would have them read *Tom Jones*, because "the Tom Jones is there in all of us who are not anaemic or consumptive." He has no use for the extreme feminist like Mrs. Spender in *The Master of Mrs. Chilvers* who would elevate women at the expense of men, but he has sympathy for the career girl, an admirable Miss Ramsbotham in *Tommy and Co.*, for example. But while wishing women better informed, more *au courant*, it is only that they may make the better helpmeet for man.

Jerome's stories or plays that deal with caste, in most cases, concern women. A woman of beauty, common sense, and a touch of flair, has every right to rise to aristocracy if she marries because of love; for cooks, music-hall girls, and tea-shop waitresses in his stories and plays marry well. When a Barbara Hasluck in *Paul Kelver* marries for position, not love, the result of her social climbing proves disastrous. In one case only, in *Anthony John* does a man from the working classes marry into a titled family; and Anthony John, after working his way to wealth and marriage, renounces his position.

Jerome's idealism becomes a pressing message in his later works. The Stranger in *The Passing of the Third Floor Back* sees good in every man, and a redeeming quality when man chooses to allow his good to prevail. In two major works, *All Roads Lead to Calvary* and *Anthony John*, Jerome formulates his idealism into a theology, patterned from Tolstoy, in which God is limited; Christ, too, is searching for God; and together Christ and man must work to aid a God who wills good but is helpless without man's choice of doing good.

The conscience of Jerome, developed in his Puritan upbringing, made him on the defensive about his humor. The Stranger in *The Passing of the Third Floor Back* must tell the entertainer Larcom that the artist is always a philanthropist, "dull, tired faces shall be made to smile. You give them—yourself." Paul Kelver must be encouraged by Norah to believe that his humor, "this fortress of laughter—this rallying-point for all the forces of joy and gladness" does good.

Jerome, despite touches of fancy—sometimes absurd romanticism—has a sense of the real that can depict not only the grim but the evil. But this same common sense can look at the literature of Realism and deflate it; for literature itself, he recognizes, is not life. The world of the theater, for all his participation in it, he sometimes sees as pitiful pretense. Jephson, closing the conversation in *Novel Notes*, says he is tired of the eternal cackle about books: "Books have their place in the world, but they are not its purpose. They are things side by side with beef and mutton, the scene of the sea, the touch of a hand, the memory of a hope. . . . Yet we speak of them as though they were the voice of life instead of merely its faint, distorted echo." Jerome's voice at the turn of the century came as near as anyone's to a non-distorted echo of the lives of masses who read him. He spoke for the genial, middle way.

II *Jerome in His Time*

Richard Le Gallienne thought that from Jerome to Beardsley was stretching the octave (presumably between sophistication and vulgarity) and that the two were seldom mentioned in the same breath. Not so, for Jerome as an editor drew to him writers (including Le Gallienne) from the esthetic movement and its opposite, the counterdecadence of "Henley's regatta," as it was called. Robert Louis Stevenson, Rudyard Kipling, Gilbert Parker, Charles Whibley, G. S. Street, George Wyndham contributed to William Ernest Henley's the *National Observer*, which was known for its iconoclasm and for Henley's truculent criticism. *The Idler* and *To-day* published stories, serialized novels, poems, and essays from writers appearing in both camps. Aubrey Beardsley is featured in a special supplement of *To-day*; Robert Louis Stevenson's *Ebb-Tide* was the pride of Jerome in his first issue of *To-day*; the realism of George Gissing appears in a story in *To-day*; and Le Gallienne, of the Rhymers' Club, and George Bernard Shaw wrote for Jerome.

Jerome preserved a near middle stance in the decade of the 1890's. *The Idler* has one poem, complete with extensive footnotes, by Robert Buchanan attacking the pessimists of literature; and Jerome attacked in *To-day* the scandalous issues of *The Chameleon* to which Oscar Wilde contributed. Jerome complimented the editors of *The Yellow Book* on its first number; but on the whole, Jerome and his young men stand closer to the Henley group, without their brutality. *The National Observer* never complimented Jerome in a review, but its writers wrote for both *The Idler* and *To-day;* and they were probably pleased not to have their work emended, as Henley was likely to do.

In the field of drama, Jerome was prolific. That he was successful is confirmed by his stellar casts, record runs, and the frequency with which his plays traveled to America or were translated for Continental performances. The subjects concerned current problems of caste, the vote, the new woman, or the plays provided situation comedy. *The Passing of the Third Floor Back* alone could have made him famous. Its worth, however, was debated immediately; reviewers like Max Beerbohm thought it tawdry; others reverenced the work as a moving, modern morality. But reviewers had little to do with audiences, and audiences loved it.

In the field of the novel, Jerome scarcely established himself. His autobiographical *Paul Kelver,* published in mid-life, perhaps excels as literature anything he wrote. The novels that followed it are either light entertainment, like *Tommy and Co.* or *They and I,* or lopsidedly didactic as in *All Roads Lead to Calvary* and *Anthony John.* Unlike Tolstoy, Jerome could not balance his ideology with his art, nor did he keep pace with the changes in the novel being initiated by the new school of James Joyce.

III   *Jerome Today*

When we examine the magazines *The Idler* and *To-day,* we are impressed with the wealth of good writing and reputable authors in their pages. But the life of periodicals is ephemeral; perhaps the best of it reappears in books. From the first, Jerome's journalistic contributions reached book form, and his *On the Stage–And Off, Three Men in a Boat, Idle Thoughts of an Idle Fellow,* and a few other collections became familiar in the households on both sides the Atlantic. Their fame, however, is fast fading. *Three Men in a Boat* remains popular. An occasional reader, picking up the *Idle Thoughts,* is surprised at how pertinent the ideas are. "A collection of light articles becomes a complete mirage," as V. S. Pritchett says. As a humorist, Jerome will probably last, for he is as much recognized outside England as in. As for his plays, they remain period pieces or comedy to be brought up to date by amateur players. Even *The Passing of the Third Floor Back* asks for a proper mood and time, or it is likely to be misplayed as melodrama. Jerome's novel *Paul Kelver* not only records a period, a temperament, and an individual, but it is a well-written novel, deserving of more fame than it has.

The twentieth century, looking back with more interest, to the literature of transition between mid-Victorianism and the Post-World-War-I movements, may well decide that Jerome K. Jerome crystallizes a large segment of the thought at the turn of the century. He stays, a humorist for all time—a "fortress of laughter."

Notes and References

Chapter One

1. *Anthony John* (New York, 1923), p. 182.
2. *John Ingerfield and Other Stories* (New York, 1894), pp. 189–90.
3. *Anthony John*, pp. 170–71.
4. *My Life and Times* (New York, 1926), p. 30.
5. *My Life and Times*, pp. 45–46.
6. *Ibid.*, p. 47.
7. *Ibid.*, p. 57.
8. *Ibid.*, p. 68.
9. For example, Michael R. Booth, *English Melodrama* (London, 1965), makes considerable use of Jerome's *On the Stage–and Off* and *Stage-Land* to document his history.
10. *My Life and Times*, p. 85.
11. *Ibid.*, p. 107.
12. Alfred Moss, *Jerome K. Jerome* (London, 1928), p. 96.
13. DeMarcus Brown directed the play at the Fallon House Theater in Columbia, Calfornia, in the summer of 1966.
14. *My Life and Times*, p. 156.
15. *Ibid.*, p. 286.
16. *Ibid.*, p. 302.
17. Since we quote extensively from this book, there is no separate criticism of *My Life and Times*.

Chapter Two

1. Sir Arthur Conan Doyle, *Memories and Adventures* (Boston, 1924), pp. 112–13.
2. *My Life and Times*, p. 74.
3. *Ibid.*, p. 80.
4. *On the Stage–and Off* (New York, 1891), p. 1. Further quotations from this book are identified by page references in the text.
5. *My Life and Times*, p. 56.

6. *Ibid.*, pp. 69–71 *passim.*

7. *Stage-Land* (New York, 1890), Dedication page.

8. *My Life and Times*, p. 83.

9. *Ibid.*, p. 107.

10. *Three Men in a Boat; Three Men on the Bummel*, Everyman's Library (London, 1966), Preface, p. x. Further quotations from this book will be identified by page references in the text.

11. *My Life and Times*, p. 108.

12. *Ibid.*, p. 109.

13. V. S. Pritchett, "The Tin-openers," *The New Statesman and Nation*, June 15, 1957, p. 783. The entire review gives an admirable analysis of Jerome's humor in *Three Men in a Boat*.

14. *Victorian Studies*, X (December, 1966), 147.

15. *The Diary of a Pilgrimage* (New York, 1891), p. 111. Further quotations from this book are identified by page references in the text.

16. It seems to me that Jerome is early in this projection of a nightmarish "Utopia."

17. *My Life and Times*, p. 76.

18. *The Idle Thoughts of an Idle Fellow* (Philadelphia, 1890), Preface, [p. 7]. Further references are indicated by page number in the text.

Chapter Three

1. *Annual Index of the "Review of Reviews"*, ed. by W. T. Stead (London, 1891), Preface, p. 1.

2. *My Life and Times*, p. 166.

3. *The Idler*, I (February 1892), 48.

4. *Annual Index*, p. 18.

5. Francis Gribble, *Seen in Passing* (London, 1929), p. 137.

6. *My Life and Times*, p. 167.

7. *Seen in Passing*, p. 137.

8. *Ibid.*, p. 134.

9. *My Life and Times*, p. 185.

10. Richard Le Gallienne in a letter of November 11, 1936, seems to disclaim close connection with Jerome: "From Jerome to Beardsley is stretching the octave indeed—and I suppose the two have seldom been mentioned in the same breath—though indeed I have quite a friendly feeling for J.K.J., particularly when I recall that he too belonged to the '90's—though not to our side of it. . . ." Quoted in *The Quest of the Golden Boy*, by Richard Whittington-Egan and Geoffrey Smerdon (London, 1960), p. 528.

11. Alfred Moss, *Jerome K. Jerome*, p. 202.

12. *My Life and Times*, p. 194.

13. *Novel Notes* (New York, 1893), Preface, p. 3. Further quotations from *Novel Notes* in this chapter are identified by page references in the text.

14. Called "The Dancing Partner," it appears in *Alfred Hitchcock Presents. The Stories They Wouldn't Let me Do on TV* (New York, 1957) and in Dorothy L. Sayers' collection *Omnibus of Crime* (New York, 1929).

15. *John Ingerfield*, pp. 204-05. Further quotations are by page references in the text.

16. *Sketches in Lavender, Blue, and Green* (New York, 1897). Further quotations will be by page number in the text.

17. *My Life and Times*, p. 178.

18. *The Second Thoughts of an Idle Fellow* (London, 1898), pp. 10–11. Further quotations are by page number in the text.

19. *Three Men in a Boat; Three Men on the Bummel*, Everyman Edition (London, New York, 1966), p. 353. Further quotations are by page references in the text.

20. *The Observations of Henry* (New York, 1901), pp. 3–4. Further quotations from this book are by page number in the text.

21. *Tea Table Talk* (London, 1903), p. 112. Further quotations from this book are by page number in the text.

22. *Idle Ideas in 1905* (London, 1905), pp. 24–25. Further quotations from this book are by page number in the text.

23. *The Passing of the Third Floor Back—and Other Stories* (London, 1907), p. 3. Further quotations from this book are by page number in the text.

24. *The Angel and the Author* (London, 1908), p. 35. Further quotations from this book are by page number in the text.

25. *Malvina of Brittany* (London, 1916), p. 117. Further quotations from this book are by page number in the text.

Chapter Four

1. A movie version appeared in the 1930's; it was revived in 1949 in New York; in 1966 DeMarcus Brown produced the play at the Fallon House Theater in Columbia, California.

2. One of the chapters, "How to Get a Play Accepted," appears anonymously in the Dec. 23, 1893, issue of *To-day*.

3. *My Life and Times*, p. 137.

4. (Cambridge, 1949), I, 186.

5. *Playhouse Impressions* (London, 1892), pp. 168–72.

6. *Our Theatres in the Nineties*, Vol. II (New York, 1931), 109. Further references to Shaw's criticism in this chapter are from this, the Ayot St. Lawrence edition of the collected works, and will be referred to by volume and page numbers in the text.

7. *My Life and Times*, p. 132.

8. *Ibid.*, p. 155.

9. Alan S. Downer, *The British Drama* (New York, 1950), pp. 281 and 287.

10. *My Life and Times*, p. 146.

11. *Ibid.*, pp. 145–46.

12. *Ibid.*, p. 157.

13. Reprinted from *Harper's* in *The Angel and the Author*.

14. *Punch*, September 9, 1908, p. 186.

15. *Around Theatres* (New York, 1954), pp. 517, 519.

16. *The Forum*, XL (November 1909), 440.

17. *My Life and Times*, p. 165.

18. *Miss Hobbs* (New York, 1902), p. 13. Further references to this play are indicated by page number in the text.

19. The 1967 London revival of Shaw's play proved surprisingly good entertainment and had a successful run and good reviews.

20. *Fanny and the Servant Problem* (New York, 1909), p. 40. Further quotations from this play are indicated by page number in the text.

21. *The Observations of Henry*, p. 27.

22. *The Celebrity* (New York, 1927), p. 34. Further quotations from this play are indicated by page number in the text.

23. *The Master of Mrs. Chilvers* (London, 1911), pp. vii–viii. Further quotations from this play are indicated by page number in the text.

24. *My Life and Times*, p. 6.

25. *Ibid.*, p. 8.

26. *Ibid.*, pp. 155–56.

27. *Ibid.*, p. 162.

28. *Ibid.*, p. 163.

29. *The Passing of the Third Floor Back* [story] (London, 1907), p. 4.

30. *Ibid.*, (New York, 1932), p. 196. Further quotations from this play are indicated by page numbers in the text.

31. Just possibly Shaw in *Pygmalion* (1913) may have intended to satirize the reform of a Stasia by countering with the correction of a cockney accent as more beneficial than conversion to one's better self.

Chapter Five

1. *My Life and Times*, p. 130.
2. *Ibid.*, p. 130.
3. *Paul Kelver* (London, 1902), p. 398. Further quotations are identified by page number in the text.
4. James Douglas' review of *Paul Kelver* in *The Bookman*, XVI (December 1902), 376–77, pretends the public has been deceived and that the book is a takeoff on *David Copperfield*. This view overlooks the fact that Mr. Jerome's life (and Paul's) did quite resemble Dickens' (and David's) struggles to fame. Furthermore, practically all maturation novels after *David Copperfield* owe some debt to its pattern.
5. *Tommy and Co.* (London, n. d.), p. 298. Further quotations from this book are identified by page number in the text.
6. George Gissing, who later contributed to Jerome's journal *To-day*, presented the grim side of the journalistic struggle in *New Grub Street* (1891), also a *roman à clef*.
7. *They and I* (London, n. d.), p. 176. Further quotations are identified by page number in the text.
8. Moss' initial remarks that this work "can hardly be called a novel in the general acceptance of the term" because it combines fiction with politics (p. 179 in *Jerome K. Jerome*) has possibly misled bibliographers. *The Cambridge Bibliography of English Literature* lists this work under Jerome's non-fiction rather than with his novels. There is no question but that *All Roads Lead to Calvary* is a novel.
9. Moss, *Jerome K. Jerome*, p. 182.
10. *All Roads Lead to Calvary* (New York, 1919), p. 20. Further quotations from this work are indicated by page numbers in the text.
11. The copy of *All Roads Lead to Calvary* borrowed for this study from the public library of a large California city, however, shows a continuous circulation on the one card from 1938 to the present.
12. *Anthony John* (New York, 1923), p. 276. Further quotations are indicated by page numbers in the text.

Selected Bibliography

PRIMARY SOURCES

Editions listed below are the ones used in this study and not necessarily first editions.

1. Novels:

Paul Kelver. London: Hutchinson and Co., 1902.
Tommy and Co. London: Hutchinson and Co., undated. Fourth edition [1904].
They and I. London: Hutchinson and Co., undated [1909].
All Roads Lead to Calvary. New York: Dodd, Mead and Co., 1919.
Anthony John. New York: Dodd, Mead and Co., 1923.

2. Periodicals Edited.

The Idler Magazine. Edited by Jerome K. Jerome and Robert Barr from February, 1892, to July, 1894. Edited by Jerome K. Jerome from August, 1894, to November, 1897.
To-day. A Weekly Magazine-Journal. Edited by Jerome K. Jerome from November 11, 1893, to October 30, 1897.

3. Miscellaneous Volumes: Humor, Short Stories, Essays, Autobiography.

On the Stage–And Off. New York: Henry Holt and Co., 1891.
Stage-Land. New York: Henry Holt and Co., 1890.
The Humours of Cycling. London: Chatto and Windus, 1905. Chapter, "Women and Wheels," by Jerome K. Jerome.
Three Men in a Boat (To Say Nothing of the Dog). New York: Dutton. Everyman's Library. 1966.
The Idle Thoughts of an Idle Fellow. Philadelphia: Henry Altemus, 1890.
Told After Supper. London: The Leadenhall Press, 1891.
Diary of a Pilgrimage (And Six Essays). New York: Henry Holt and Co., 1891.
Novel Notes. New York: Henry Holt and Co., 1893.

John Ingerfield (And Other Stories). New York: Henry Holt and
    Co., 1894.
Sketches in Lavender, Blue, and Green. New York: Henry Holt
    and Co., 1897.
The Second Thoughts of an Idle Fellow. London: Hurst and
    Blackett, Ltd., 1898.
Three Men on The Bummel (Printed with *Three Men in a Boat*),
    supra.
The Observations of Henry. New York: Dodd, Mead and Co.,
    1901.
Tea Table Talk. London: Hutchinson and Co., 1903.
American Wives and Others. New York: Frederick A. Stokes Co.,
    1904.
Idle Ideas in 1905. London: Hurst and Blackett, Ltd. [1905].
    [Same as item above]
The Passing of the Third Floor Back (And Other Stories). London:
    Hurst and Blackett, Ltd., 1907.
The Angel and the Author (And Others). London: Hurst and
    Blackett, Ltd., 1908.
Malvina of Brittany. London: Cassell and Co., Ltd., 1916.
The Street of the Blank Wall. New York: Dodd, Mead and Co.,
    1917. [Same as item above]
My Life and Times. New York: Harper and Brothers, 1926.

4. Plays. If the publisher is not listed, the dates refer to stage pro-
    duction of the play.

Barbara. London: Samuel French, 1886.
Sunset. New York: Fitzgerald Publishing Corp., undated.
Fennel. New York: Samuel French, undated. [from François
    Coppée's *Le Luthier de Crémone*]
Woodbarrow Farm. London: Samuel French, 1904.
Pity is Akin to Love. 1888.
New Lamps for Old. 1890.
Ruth [in collaboration with Addison Bright]. 1890.
What Women Will Do. 1890.
Honour. 1890. [adapted from Sudermann's *Die Ehre*]. In Scot-
    land, produced as *Birth and Breeding*.
The Prude's Progress [in collaboration with Eden Phillpotts].
    London: Samuel French, 1895. In America, *The Councillor's
    Wife*, 1892.
The Rise of Dick Halward. 1895.
Biarritz [in collaboration with A. Ross]. 1896.

The MacHaggis [in collaboration with Eden Phillpotts]. 1897.
Miss Hobbs. New York: Samuel French, 1902.
John Ingerfield. 1899.
Tommy. undated. [an adaptation of *Tommy and Co.*]
The Passing of the Third Floor Back. New York: Samuel French, 1932.
Fanny and the Servant Problem. New York: Samuel French, 1909. In America, *The New Lady Bantock.* Possibly the musical comedy *The Rainbow Girl.*
The Master of Mrs. Chilvers. London: T. Fisher Unwin, 1911.
When Greek Meets Greek. Philadelphia: The Penn Publishing Co., 1913.
Poor Little Thing. 1914. [adapted from Jules Lemaître]
The Great Gamble. 1914.
Robina in Search of a Husband. London: Samuel French, 1914. In America, *Susan in Search of a Husband.* 1906.
The Celebrity. New York: Samuel French, 1927. Same as *Cook.*
The Soul of Nicholas Snyders. London: Hodder and Stoughton, 1925. In America, *Man or Devil.*

5. Collections of humor.

A Miscellany of Sense and Nonsense from the Writings of Jerome K. Jerome. New York: Dodd, Mead and Company, 1924. [Jerome's own selection]
The Humorous World of Jerome K. Jerome, edited and with an introduction by Robert Hutchinson. New York: Dover Publications, 1962.

6. Anonymous publication.

Playwriting: A Handbook for Would-be Dramatic Authors. London: The Stage Office, 189?.

SECONDARY SOURCES

1. Published dissertations.

BOSSOM, OLAF E. *Slang and Cant in Jerome K. Jerome's Works.* Cambridge: W. Heffer and Sons, 1911.
GUTKESS, WALTER. *Jerome K. Jerome. Seine Persönlichkeit und literarische Bedeutung.* Jena: Walter Biedermann, 1930.
WOLFENSBERGER, MAGNUS. *Jerome K. Jerome. Sein literarisches Werk.* Zurich, 1953.

2. Biography

MOSS, ALFRED. *Jerome K. Jerome*. London: Selwyn and Blount,
    1928. Based on Jerome's autobiographical *My Life and Times*
    with additional interviews and letters by people whom Jerome
    knew. More organized than Jerome's work, but lacks his style.
DOYLE, SIR ARTHUR CONAN. *Memories and Adventures*. Boston:
    Little, Brown, and Co., 1924. Contains references to Jerome's
    personality and their friendship.
KERNAHAN, COULSON. *Celebrities*. London: Hutchinson and Co.,
    1923. Ten-page chapter of reminiscences.
GRIBBLE, FRANCIS. *Seen in Passing*. London: Ernest Been, Ltd.,
    1929. More reminiscences, with some information on "The
    Idler at homes."
WHITTINGTON-EGAN, RICHARD, and GEOFFREY MERDON. *The Quest
    of the Golden Boy*. London: The Unicorn Press, 1960. Life and
    letters of Richard Le Gallienne containing mention of Jerome
    in two or three letters.
WOHLGELERNTER, MAURICE. *Israel Zangwill*. New York: Colum-
    bia University Press, 1964. Some information on the "new
    humor" and Jerome's peace movement efforts.

3. Reviews of particular books or plays.

The Baron de Book-worm. "Our Booking-Office," *Punch* (Febru-
    ary 1, 1890). Review of *Three Men in a Boat* comparing it
    unfavorably with *Pickwick;* (January 3, 1891). Review of *Told
    After Supper*, laments Yankee humor and failure to rise to
    Dickens' level; (May 16, 1891). Review of *Diary of a Pilgrimage*,
    dismissed briefly as 'Arry abroad.
BEERBLOCK, MAURICE. "Jerome K. Jerome," *Revue Générale Belge*
    (May 1959). Centenary article; complimentary to Jerome.
BEERBOHM, MAX. "A Deplorable Affair." *Around Theatres*. New
    York: Simon and Schuster, 1954. Devastating review of *The
    Passing of the Third Floor Back* and condemnation of the pub-
    lic for liking it.
"A British Drama of Our 'Society'," *The Literary Digest*, XLVI
    (February 22, 1913), 401. Unfavorable review of *Esther Cast-
    ways*.
DOUGLAS, JAMES. "Mr. Jerome's *Paul Kelver*," *The Bookman*, XVI
    (December 1902), 376–77. Insists the book a satire on *David
    Copperfield*. Scornful.
HAMILTON, CLAYTON. "Imitation and Suggestion in the Drama,"

The Forum, XLII (November 1909), 220–21. Favorable review of *The Passing of the Third Floor Back.*

"Humour of Jerome," *The Bookman*, XI (July 1900), 410–11. Review of *Three Men on Wheels*, "not at all bad reading for the lazy months of the year."

PRITCHETT, V. S. "The Tin-openers," *The New Statesman and Nation* (June 15, 1957), pp. 783–84. Superb review of *Three Men in a Boat* and of Jeromian humor.

S[EAMAN], O[WEN]. "At the Play," *Punch* (September 9, 1908). Review of *The Passing of the Third Floor Back*, reluctantly complimentary; (October 21, 1908). Not unfavourable review of *Fanny and the Servant Problem.*

SHAW, GEORGE BERNARD. *Our Theatre in the Nineties.* Three volumes. Wm. H. Wise, and Co., 1931. Reviews, favorable and unfavorable in Shavian wit of *Biarritz, The Rise of Dick Halward, The Prude's Progress, The MacHaggis.* Entertaining and perceptive—worth reading.

WALKLEY, A. B. "J. K. Jerome." *Playhouse Impressions.* London: T. F. Unwin, 1892. Reviews of *New Lamps for Old* and *Woodbarrow Farm.* Claims Jerome lacks originality.

WEALES, GERALD CLIFFORD. *Religion in Modern English Drama.* Philadelphia: University of Pennsylvania Press, 1961. Two page discussion, "The Sentimental Supernaturalism" (38, 39) of *The Passing of the Third Floor Back* and *The Soul of Nicholas Snyders.* The tone is belittling.

4. Brief mention of Jerome and background of the theater of his time.

BAILEY, J. O. *British Plays of the Nineteenth Century.* New York: The Odyssey Press, 1966. Good anthology of the popular drama.

BOOTH, MICHAEL. *English Melodrama.* London: Herbert Jenkins, 1965. Uses Jerome's illustrations for the discussion of the melodrama of the time.

DOWNER, ALAN S. *The British Drama.* New York: Appleton-Century-Crofts, Inc. 1950. Good brief history.

FELHEIM, MARVIN. *The Theater of Augustin Daly.* Cambridge: Harvard University Press, 1956. Mention of Jerome's and Daly's adaptations.

MANTLE, BURNS and GARRISON P. SHERWOOD. *The Best Plays of 1899* [and subsequent years to 1925]. New York: Dodd, Mead and Co., 1944. Indispensable information on productions and casts.

MILLET, FRED B. and GERALD EADES BENTLEY. *The Art of the Drama.* New York: D. Appleton-Century Co., 1935. Standard.

NICOLL, ALLARDYCE. *A History of Late Nineteenth Century Drama.* Cambridge: Cambridge University Press, 1949. Authoritative.

————. *English Drama, 1900–1930.* Cambridge: Cambridge University Press, 1973. Favorable comments on Jerome's *The Passing of the Third Floor Back.* Survey of entire period of drama.

ODELL, GEORGE C. D. *Annals of the New York Stage.* New York: Columbia University Press. Mention of Jerome's plays in America.

PEARSON, HESKETH. *Extraordinary People.* New York: Harper and Row, 1965. Chapter on Sir Johnston Forbes-Robertson mentions his role in *The Passing of the Third Floor Back.*

REYNOLDS, ERNEST. *Modern English Drama from 1900.* Norman, Oklahoma: University of Oklahoma Press, 1951. Continues Nicoll's work into the twentieth century.

TENNANT, PETER F. D. *Ibsen's Dramatic Technique.* New York: Humanities Press, 1965.

5. Other useful background studies.

BUCKLEY, JEROME HAMILTON. *William Ernest Henley. A Study in the "Counter-Decadence" of the Nineties.* Princeton, New Jersey: Princeton University Press, 1945. Valuable study of rival of Jerome's *The Idler* and journalists of the period.

CORRIGAN, ROBERT W., ed. *Comedy. Meaning and Form.* San Francisco: Chandler Publishing Co., 1965. An anthology; contains many essays on humor.

CROFT-COOKE, RUPERT. *Feasting With Panthers.* New York: Holt, Rinehart and Winston, 1967. Brief mention of the "jolly humourists."

GISSING, GEORGE. *New Grub Street.* London: The Bodley Head, 1967. Novel on the grim side of journalism.

GRAY, DONALD J. "The Uses of Victorian Laughter," *Victorian Studies,* X (December 1966), 145–76. With the following item, a good analysis of Victorian humor though no mention of Jerome.

SUTTON, MAX KEITH. " 'Inverse Sublimity' in Victorian Humor," *Victorian Studies,* X (December 1966), 177–92.

Index